5th International Workshop on Search-Oriented Conversational AI (SCAI 2020)

Online
19 November 2020

ISBN: 978-1-7138-2002-4

Printed from e-media with permission by:

Curran Associates, Inc.
57 Morehouse Lane
Red Hook, NY 12571

Some format issues inherent in the e-media version may also appear in this print version.

Association for Computational Linguistics
209 N. Eighth Street
Stroudsburg, Pennsylvania 18360

Phone: 1-570-476-8006
Fax: 1-570-476-0860

acl@aclweb.org

Additional copies of this publication are available from:

Curran Associates, Inc.
57 Morehouse Lane
Red Hook, NY 12571 USA
Phone: 845-758-0400
Fax: 845-758-2633
Email: curran@proceedings.com
Web: www.proceedings.com

EMNLP 2020

Search-Oriented Conversational AI (SCAI)

Proceedings of the 5th International Workshop on Search-Oriented Conversational AI (SCAI):

November 19, 2020
Online

Competition Sponsors

Microsoft

amazon | science

Google

Introduction

Welcome to the the 5th International Workshop on Search-Oriented Conversational AI. Following the success of the previous four installments, the workshop is coming back to EMNLP this year. Like the rest of the conference, the workshop will be run fully online this year.

This year we received six valid submissions for the main workshop track and accepted three of them. That yields an acceptance rate of 50%, similar to those of previous years (59% in 2018 and 57% in 2019). We also considered several topically relevant EMNLP Findings papers for non-archival oral presentation and accepted at least two of them (see online program for the full list).

In additon, this year we have hosted a new edition of Conversational Intelligence Challenge on Clarifying Questions for Open-Domain Dialogue Systems (ClariQ), where we have 8 active teams who participated.

Jeff Dalton, Aleksandr Chuklin, Julia Kiseleva, and Mikhail Burtsev

Organizers:

Jeff Dalton, University of Glasgow
Aleksandr Chuklin, Google Research
Julia Kiseleva, Microsoft Research
Mikhail Burtsev, MIPT

Conversational Challenge:

Mohammad Aliannejadi, University of Amsterdam (Challenge Chair)
Gustavo Penha, TU Delft

Program Committee:

Damiano Spina, RMIT University (Australia)
Igor Shalyminov, Heriot-Watt University (UK)
Jaap Kamps, University of Amsterdam (The Netherlands)
Tom Kenter, Google (UK)
Scott Roy, Google (USA)

Invited Speakers:

Y-Lan Boureau, Facebook AI Research
Thomas Wolf, Hugging Face
Verena Rieser, Heriot Watt University
Ivan Vulic, PolyAI
Sungjin Lee, Amazon
Jason Weston, Facebook AI Research
Jian-Yun Nie, Université de Montréal

Table of Contents

Conference Program

Slice-Aware Neural Ranking
Gustavo Penha and Claudia Hauff

A Wrong Answer or a Wrong Question? An Intricate Relationship between Question Reformulation and Answer Selection in Conversational Question Answering
Svitlana Vakulenko, Shayne Longpre, Zhucheng Tu and Raviteja Anantha

Multi-Task Learning using Dynamic Task Weighting for Conversational Question Answering
Sarawoot Kongyoung, Craig Macdonald and Iadh Ounis

EMNLP Findings Presentations:
Semantically Driven Sentence Fusion: Modeling and Evaluation
Eyal Ben-David, Orgad Keller, Eric Malmi, Idan Szpektor and Roi Reichart

Toward Stance-based Personas for Opinionated Dialogues
Thomas Scialom, Serra Sinem Tekiroğlu, Jacopo Staiano and Marco Guerini

* The list above was compiled on October 15, 2020 and may be incomplete. Please refer to the workshop website https://scai.info/2020/ for a complete program.

Slice-Aware Neural Ranking

Gustavo Penha
TU Delft
g.penha-1@tudelft.nl

Claudia Hauff
TU Delft
c.hauff@tudelft.nl

Abstract

Understanding when and why neural ranking models fail for an IR task via error analysis is an important part of the research cycle. Here we focus on the challenges of (i) identifying categories of *difficult* instances (a pair of question and response candidates) for which a neural ranker is ineffective and (ii) improving neural ranking for such instances. To address both challenges we resort to *slice-based learning* (Chen et al., 2019) for which the goal is to improve effectiveness of neural models for slices (subsets) of data. We address challenge (i) by proposing different *slicing functions* (SFs) that select slices of the dataset—based on prior work we heuristically capture different failures of neural rankers. Then, for challenge (ii) we adapt a neural ranking model to learn slice-aware representations, i.e. the adapted model learns to represent the question and responses differently based on the model's prediction of which slices they belong to. Our experimental results[1] across three different ranking tasks and four corpora show that slice-based learning improves the effectiveness by an average of 2% over a neural ranker that is not slice-aware.

1 Introduction

Retrieving text for a given information need is a fundamental task in Information Retrieval (IR). For a long time neural networks failed to convincingly outperform traditional term matching approaches with pseudo-relevance feedback, e.g. RM3 (Abdul-Jaleel et al., 2004), for text retrieval tasks including the classic adhoc retrieval task (Yang et al., 2019a). However, with recent breakthroughs in natural language processing (NLP), neural approaches—prominently BERT (Devlin et al., 2019)—are achieving state-of-the-art effectiveness across a

[1]The source code and data are available at https://github.com/Guzpenha/slice_based_learning.

SF_0

```
def sf_long_question(x, t=5):
    return len(x.question.split(" ")) > t
```

SF_1

```
def sf_BERT_difficulty(x, t=0.1):
    p_rel = np.mean([BERT.pred(x.question, res) \
                     for res in x.rel_resp])
    p_not_rel = np.mean([BERT.pred(x.question, res)\
                     for res in x.not_rel_resp])
    return (p_rel - p_not_rel) < t
```

Figure 1: Examples of slicing functions (SFs) to capture subsets of difficult tuples of question and response list. The SFs also have access to relevance labels for the training set, as they are not required at test time by the slice-aware neural ranker. SF_0 uses the question length as a proxy for question complexity, and SF_1 calculates how distinguishable relevant and non-relevant responses are based on BERT predictions.

range of text retrieval tasks (Yang et al., 2019b; Nogueira and Cho, 2019).

Understanding when and why retrieval models fail is an important part of the research cycle. Even tough we have clues about the failures of neural rankers—obtained for instance by the study of question performance prediction (He and Ounis, 2006), diagnostic datasets (Câmara and Hauff, 2020) and error analysis (Wu et al., 2019)—automatically identifying difficult instances (tuples of question and response list) and improving the effectiveness of models for such difficult instances are still open challenges. We consider here difficult instances to be question and responses for which a given neural ranker retrieval effectiveness is below the average. A recent approach, referred to as *slice-based learning* (Chen et al., 2019), has been proposed to identify and improve the effectiveness of subsets of data (so-called *slices*), as opposed to focusing on all data equally. The core idea is that a slice-aware neural model will represent instances differently depending on the slices of data they come from. Slice-based learning has been applied to computer vision and NLP tasks, with overall effectiveness improvements up to 3.5% (Chen et al., 2019) over a model that is not slice-aware.

In this paper we focus on the challenges of (i)

Proceedings of the 5th International Workshop on Search-Oriented Conversational AI (SCAI), pages 1–6
Online, November 19, 2020.

detecting difficult instances for neural rankers and (ii) improving the retrieval effectiveness for such instances. We address the challenges by (i) creating slicing functions (SFs), i.e., functions that define whether an instance belongs to a slice which heuristically capture different errors of rankers (cf. Figure 2 for examples of SFs); and (ii) employing a slice-aware neural ranker, i.e., a neural ranker that learns to represent each instance differently based on its prediction of which slice the input belongs to (cf. Figure 2 for a diagram of the slice-aware neural ranker). Our main research questions are the following two. **RQ1:** To what extent can slice-based learning improve neural ranking models? **RQ2**: What are the underlying reasons for the effectiveness of slice-based learning?

Our experimental results on three different conversational tasks show that slice-based learning is beneficial to IR, showing positive evidence for RQ1. The gains are observed for both overall effectiveness and the effectiveness for slices of the data. Concerning RQ2, we evaluate to which extent the effectiveness gains observed for the slice-aware model come from the effect of ensemble learning (Dietterich et al., 2002), a direction not explored empirically by previous work (Chen et al., 2019). We find that, when using *random* SFs we can also significantly improve upon a non slice-aware neural ranker. We note though that not all improvements of slice-based learning can be attributed to the effect of ensemble learning, and carefully implementing SFs is indeed advantageous.

2 Slice-based Learning

Slice-based learning (Chen et al., 2019) is an approach based on the engineering of SFs that capture slices of data. The SFs all follow the same format: they receive the instance as input (in our case a question and a list of candidate responses) and return a boolean variable indicating whether the instance belongs to the slice. Based on the SFs a neural model is adapted to improve the effectiveness of such slices of data, for example, by having a different set of weights for each slice. Training a different model for each slice, and combining their predictions is inefficient: training and maintaining a different neural ranking model for each slicing function amounts to a large number of parameters and an increased prediction time. As an efficient solution, Chen et al. (2019) proposed Slice-Residual-Attention Modules (SRAMs), which is a

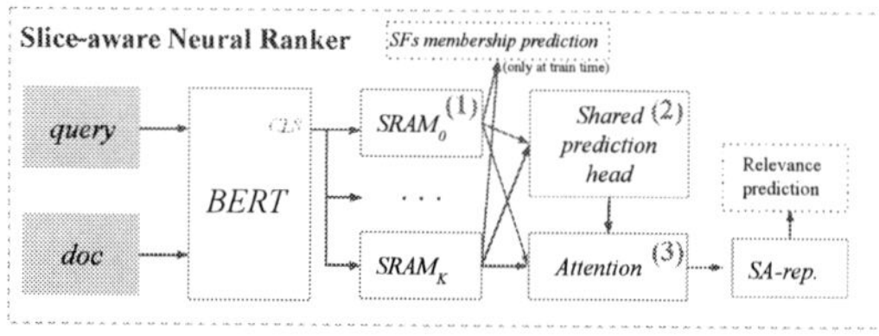

Figure 2: Overview of the slice-aware neural ranker. For each SF we define we have a SRAM module to learn slice-expert representations, that are then combined with an attention mechanism into a slice-aware representation.

slice-aware approach for neural models that shares parameters in a similar manner to multi-task learning (Caruana, 1997).

3 Slice-based learning for IR

We first introduce the SFs we defined to heuristically capture subsets of data containing different categories of errors, for which the effectiveness is lower than average, based on intuitions drawn from prior work (RQ1). We then introduce the random SFs we deploy to study the effect of ensemble learning in slice-based learning (RQ2). Finally we describe the slice-aware neural ranker.

3.1 Slicing Functions

We divide our SFs into two categories: those based only on the question text (question based) and those that uses both the question and the list of candidate responses (question-responses based). The relevance labels for the training instances are also inputs to the SFs, which are not required at inference time as the slice-aware neural ranker learns to predict slice-membership.

3.1.1 Question-based SFs

Question Length (QL): the number of question terms is higher than the threshold T_{QL}. QL was shown to correlate negatively with the effectiveness of retrieval methods in adhoc retrieval (Bendersky and Croft, 2009). Long questions (questions with high QL) provide a way of expressing complex information needs as opposed to short questions (Phan et al., 2007). Context Length (CL) [2]: the number of turns in the dialogue context is higher than the threshold T_{CL}. CL was shown to correlate negatively with model's effectiveness for the conversation response ranking task when using different neural rankers (Tao et al., 2019).

[2]This SF is only suited for QA tasks with multiple turns.

Question Category (QC): question is about a certain semantic category, e.g. $QC = travel$ selects questions about travel. Knowing which topic a question belongs to can lead to retrieval effectiveness improvements, for instance by using federated search (Shokouhi and Si, 2011), intent-aware ranking (Glater et al., 2017) or multi-task learning (Liu et al., 2015). Instances from different categories could display different effectiveness values, e.g. questions about *physics* could be a potential difficult category. Question type (5W1H): a categorization into types of question (who, what, where, when, why, how), e.g. $5W1H = what$ selects *what* questions. 5W1H has been used to inform dialogue management modules (Han et al., 2013). The type of question can yield different models' effectiveness (Kim et al., 2019).

3.1.2 Question-Responses based SFs

Question Response Term Match (QDTM): The number of words that appear in both the question and a relevant response is smaller than the threshold T_{QDTM}. The difference in vocabulary, i.e. lexical gap, between queries and documents has shown to be a problem in IR (Lee et al., 2008) and has to lead to remedies such as query expansion (Voorhees, 1994) and the use of neural ranking models for semantic matching (Guo et al., 2019). Responses Lexical Similarity (DLS): average TF-IDF similarity between the top-k most similar responses in the candidate list to the relevant response is higher than the threshold T_{DLS}. The amount of internal coherence, i.e. similarity between responses, has been used to predict query difficulty (He et al., 2008). The SFs can be easily extended for multiple relevant responses, e.g. by using the average or considering one representative relevant response.

3.1.3 Random SFs

The random SF randomly samples $X\%$ of the training data, where X is a hyperparameter.

3.2 Slice-Aware Neural Ranker

Figure 2 displays a diagram of the slice-aware neural ranker. Based on a backbone (BERT) that learns a representation of the question and response concatenation, the slice-aware neural ranker learns to (1) predict how much each instance belongs to each of the k slices or not (supervision is based on the boolean output of the k SFs)[3]; has k slice expert representations with its own set of weights trained using a shared prediction head (2) which predicts relevance for the question and response combination using only instances of the slice k; and (3) combines all representations from the SRAMs using attention into a single slice-aware representation that is used to make the final relevance prediction. The SFs are only used during training and thus are not needed at inference time. This is an adaptation of SRAMs (Chen et al., 2019), and the backbone could be replaced by any other neural ranker.

4 Experimental Setup

We employ four datasets and three retrieval tasks: `MSDialog` (Qu et al., 2018) and `MANtIS` (Penha et al., 2019) for conversation response ranking, `Quora` (Iyer et al., 2017) for similar question retrieval and `ANTIQUE` (Hashemi et al., 2019) for non-factoid question answering. We use the official train, validation and test sets provided by the datasets' creators. As a strong neural ranking baseline model we fine-tune BERT [4] for sentence classification, using the CLS token to predict whether the concatenation of a question and response is relevant or not, following recent research in IR (Nogueira and Cho, 2019; Yang et al., 2019b). Using 512 input tokens (larger inputs are truncated) and a batch size of 8 we train each model for 5 epochs.

When employing SRAMs (Chen et al., 2019) with a BERT backbone for neural ranking using both the question-based and question-responses based SFs we refer to the model as BERT-SA. When using random SFs we refer to the model as BERT-SA-R. For the SFs that have a threshold value (e.g., QL), we choose thresholds that select less than 50% of the data to avoid selecting the majority of the training instances in each slice. For SFs that include a categorical value, e.g., question category (QC) *physics*, we add one slice per category in the dataset. For the random SFs we create 10 different slices[5] for which 50% of randomly chosen instances from the training data belong to[6]. We train each model 5 times with different random seeds and report the test set effectiveness using Mean Average Precision (MAP). ΔMAP indicates the difference between BERT-SA(`-R`) and BERT

[3]The model has an extra SF that all instances belong to, so every instance will always belong to at least to this slice.

[4]*bert-base-uncased* with default hyperparameters (Wolf et al., 2019).

[5]Initial experiments varying the number of SFs showed a validation plateau around 10.

[6]Initial experiments varying revealed that only small percentages, less than 20%, degraded the effectiveness.

Table 1: Average of 5 runs for slice-based learning. Superscript † denote statistically significant improvements over the baseline (BERT) where no slice-based learning is applied at 95% confidence interval using Student's t-tests. Bold indicates the highest MAP for each dataset.

		Dev	Test		
		MAP (std)	MAP (std)	slice Δ MAP	
Dataset	Model			Avg.	Max.
	BERT	0.853 (.026)	0.850 (.015)	-	-
ANTIQUE	BERT-SA-R	0.874 (.025)†	0.877 (.005)†	0.028	0.063
	BERT-SA	**0.878 (.024)**†	**0.883 (.005)**†	0.035	0.112
	BERT	0.655 (.006)	0.684 (.006)	-	-
MANtIS_50	BERT-SA-R	0.671 (.006)†	**0.690 (.014)**†	0.025	0.035
	BERT-SA	**0.702 (.006)**†	0.689 (.022)†	0.025	0.034
	BERT	0.754 (.010)	0.830 (.002)	-	-
MSDialog	BERT-SA-R	**0.815 (.009)**†	**0.840 (.011)**†	0.028	0.084
	BERT-SA	0.810 (.009)†	0.818 (.010)	-0.004	0.067
	BERT	0.799 (.037)	0.819 (.008)	-	-
Quora	BERT-SA-R	0.819 (.035)†	0.837 (.004)	0.011	0.038
	BERT-SA	**0.834 (.034)**†	**0.840 (.007)**†	0.019	0.065

for the slices defined by the SFs.

5 Results

Let us first consider RQ1. We observe in Table 1 that with the exception of MSDialog, BERT-SA significantly improves over the baseline (BERT) for both the overall (column MAP) and per slice performance (column slice ΔMAP). **This demonstrates that slice-based learning is useful for neural ranking, with gains up to 3.8% overall and up to 13% per slice in terms of MAP.**

To better understand which features of a slice correlate the most with the observed gains from BERT-SA, we study how three properties of the slices correlate with the slice ΔMAP (i.e., the improvement over BERT): we consider (1) the size of the slice, (2) the classification accuracy of the slice-aware model to predict slice membership, and, (3) the BERT model effectiveness for each slice. The only property that has a statistically significant Pearson correlation (0.504 average for the different datasets) with MAP gains is the BERT baseline performance , suggesting that focusing on failures of neural ranking models (slices for which BERT has low effectiveness) when implementing SFs is effective.

To provide insights into the underlying reasons of the effectiveness of slice-based learning (RQ2), we replace the SFs that capture error categories with random SFs, i.e. BERT-SA-R. We find that this model also has a significantly better effectiveness than the BERT baseline, with the exception of Quora. **This indicates that part of the gains provided by slice-based learning could be attributed to the effect of ensemble learning**, since each slice-aware representation is trained on random parts of the data and are then combined[7]. We note however that the slice gains of BERT-SA are higher than BERT-SA-R for ANTIQUE and Quora with statistical significance. This indicates that not all improvements of slice-based learning can be attributed to the effect of ensemble learning and carefully implementing SFs is advantageous.

6 Conclusion

In this paper we demonstrated that a slice-aware neural ranker is an effective approach to IR, increasing the effectiveness of rankers by margins up to 3.8% overall and up to 13% per slice in terms of MAP. As future work we plan to study slice-aware neural rankers that do listwise optimization—such a ranker could learn better representations particularly for SFs that uses several responses as input.

[7] Another potential reason for the success of slice-based learning could be the capacity obtained by the additional number of weights compared to the baseline (e.g. from 110M to 116M for MANtIS).

Acknowledgements

This research has been supported by NWO projects SearchX (639.022.722) and NWO Aspasia (015.013.027).

References

Nasreen Abdul-Jaleel, James Allan, W Bruce Croft, Fernando Diaz, Leah Larkey, Xiaoyan Li, Mark D Smucker, and Courtney Wade. 2004. Umass at trec 2004: Novelty and hard. *Computer Science Department Faculty Publication Series*, page 189.

Michael Bendersky and W Bruce Croft. 2009. Analysis of long queries in a large scale search log. In *Workshop on Web Search Click Data*, pages 8–14.

Arthur Câmara and Claudia Hauff. 2020. Diagnosing bert with retrieval heuristics. In *European Conference on Information Retrieval*, pages 605–618. Springer.

Rich Caruana. 1997. Multitask learning. *Machine learning*, 28(1):41–75.

Vincent Chen, Sen Wu, Alexander J Ratner, Jen Weng, and Christopher Ré. 2019. Slice-based learning: A programming model for residual learning in critical data slices. In *NeurIPS*, pages 9392–9402.

Jacob Devlin, Ming-Wei Chang, Kenton Lee, and Kristina Toutanova. 2019. BERT: Pre-training of Deep Bidirectional Transformers for Language Understanding. In *NAACL*, pages 4171–4186.

Thomas G Dietterich et al. 2002. Ensemble learning. *The handbook of brain theory and neural networks*, 2:110–125.

Rafael Glater, Rodrygo LT Santos, and Nivio Ziviani. 2017. Intent-aware semantic query annotation. In *SIGIR*, pages 485–494.

Jiafeng Guo, Yixing Fan, Liang Pang, Liu Yang, Qingyao Ai, Hamed Zamani, Chen Wu, W Bruce Croft, and Xueqi Cheng. 2019. A deep look into neural ranking models for information retrieval. *arXiv preprint arXiv:1903.06902*.

Sangdo Han, Kyusong Lee, Donghyeon Lee, and Gary Geunbae Lee. 2013. Counseling dialog system with 5w1h extraction. In *SIGDIAL*, pages 349–353.

Helia Hashemi, Mohammad Aliannejadi, Hamed Zamani, and W Bruce Croft. 2019. Antique: A non-factoid question answering benchmark. *arXiv preprint arXiv:1905.08957*.

Ben He and Iadh Ounis. 2006. Query performance prediction. *Information Systems*, 31(7):585–594.

Jiyin He, Martha Larson, and Maarten De Rijke. 2008. Using coherence-based measures to predict query difficulty. In *ECIR*, pages 689–694. Springer.

Shankar Iyer, Nikhil Dandekar, and Kornél Csernai. 2017. First quora dataset release: Question pairs. *data. quora. com*.

Najoung Kim, Roma Patel, Adam Poliak, Alex Wang, Patrick Xia, R Thomas McCoy, Ian Tenney, Alexis Ross, Tal Linzen, Benjamin Van Durme, et al. 2019. Probing what different nlp tasks teach machines about function word comprehension. *arXiv preprint arXiv:1904.11544*.

Jung-Tae Lee, Sang-Bum Kim, Young-In Song, and Hae-Chang Rim. 2008. Bridging lexical gaps between queries and questions on large online q&a collections with compact translation models. In *EMNLP*, pages 410–418.

Xiaodong Liu, Jianfeng Gao, Xiaodong He, Li Deng, Kevin Duh, and Ye-Yi Wang. 2015. Representation learning using multi-task deep neural networks for semantic classification and information retrieval.

Rodrigo Nogueira and Kyunghyun Cho. 2019. Passage re-ranking with bert. *arXiv preprint arXiv:1901.04085*.

Gustavo Penha, Alexandru Balan, and Claudia Hauff. 2019. Introducing MANtIS: a novel Multi-Domain Information Seeking Dialogues Dataset. *arXiv preprint arXiv:1912.04639*.

Nina Phan, Peter Bailey, and Ross Wilkinson. 2007. Understanding the relationship of information need specificity to search query length. In *SIGIR*, pages 709–710.

Chen Qu, Liu Yang, W Bruce Croft, Johanne R Trippas, Yongfeng Zhang, and Minghui Qiu. 2018. Analyzing and characterizing user intent in information-seeking conversations. In *SIGIR*, pages 989–992.

Milad Shokouhi and Luo Si. 2011. Federated search. *Foundations and Trends® in Information Retrieval*, 5(1):1–102.

Chongyang Tao, Wei Wu, Can Xu, Wenpeng Hu, Dongyan Zhao, and Rui Yan. 2019. Multi-representation fusion network for multi-turn response selection in retrieval-based chatbots. In *WSDM*, pages 267–275.

Ellen M Voorhees. 1994. Query expansion using lexical-semantic relations. In *SIGIR*, pages 61–69.

Thomas Wolf, Lysandre Debut, Victor Sanh, Julien Chaumond, Clement Delangue, Anthony Moi, Pierric Cistac, Tim Rault, R'emi Louf, Morgan Funtowicz, and Jamie Brew. 2019. Huggingface's transformers: State-of-the-art natural language processing. *ArXiv*, abs/1910.03771.

Tongshuang Wu, Marco Tulio Ribeiro, Jeffrey Heer, and Daniel S Weld. 2019. Errudite: Scalable, reproducible, and testable error analysis. In *ACL*, pages 747–763.

Wei Yang, Kuang Lu, Peilin Yang, and Jimmy Lin. 2019a. Critically Examining theNeural Hype: Weak Baselines and the Additivity of Effectiveness Gains from Neural Ranking Models. In *SIGIR*, pages 1129–1132, New York, NY, USA.

Wei Yang, Haotian Zhang, and Jimmy Lin. 2019b. Simple applications of bert for ad hoc document retrieval. *arXiv preprint arXiv:1903.10972*.

A Wrong Answer or a Wrong Question? An Intricate Relationship between Question Reformulation and Answer Selection in Conversational Question Answering

Svitlana Vakulenko[†]
University of Amsterdam
s.vakulenko@uva.nl

Shayne Longpre, Zhucheng Tu, Raviteja Anantha
Apple Inc.
{slongpre, zhucheng_tu, raviteja_anantha}@apple.com

Abstract

The dependency between an adequate question formulation and correct answer selection is a very intriguing but still underexplored area. In this paper, we show that question rewriting (QR) of the conversational context allows to shed more light on this phenomenon and also use it to evaluate robustness of different answer selection approaches. We introduce a simple framework that enables an automated analysis of the conversational question answering (QA) performance using question rewrites, and present the results of this analysis on the TREC CAsT and QuAC (CANARD) datasets. Our experiments uncover sensitivity to question formulation of the popular state-of-the-art models for reading comprehension and passage ranking. Our results demonstrate that the reading comprehension model is insensitive to question formulation, while the passage ranking changes dramatically with a little variation in the input question. The benefit of QR is that it allows us to pinpoint and group such cases automatically. We show how to use this methodology to verify whether QA models are really learning the task or just finding shortcuts in the dataset, and better understand the frequent types of error they make.

1 Introduction

Conversational question answering (QA) is a new and important task which allows systems to advance from answering stand-alone questions to answering a sequence of related questions (Choi et al., 2018; Reddy et al., 2019; Dalton et al., 2019). Such sequences contain questions that usually revolve around the same topic and its subtopics, which is also common for a human conversation. The most pronounced characteristics of such question sequences are anaphoric expressions and ellipsis, which make the follow-up questions ambiguous outside of the conversation context. For example, consider a question "*When was **it** discovered?*". It is not possible to answer the question without resolving the pronoun **it** (example of an anaphoric expression). Ellipsis are even harder to resolve since they omit information without leaving any references. For example, a question "*When?*" can naturally follow an answer to the previous question, such as "*Friedrich Miescher discovered DNA.*"

Question rewriting (QR) was recently introduced as an independent component for conversational QA (Elgohary et al., 2019; Vakulenko et al., 2020; Yu et al., 2020). Query rewriting received considerable attention in the information retrieval community before but not in a conversational context (He et al., 2016). Ren et al. (2018) performed similar experiments using query reformulations mined from search sessions. However, half of their samples were keyword queries rather than natural language questions and their dataset was not released to the community. In this paper, we show that QR is not only operational in extending standard QA models to the conversational scenario but can be also used for their evaluation.

An input to the QR component is a question and previous conversation turns. The QR component is designed to transform all ambiguous questions, e.g., "*When?*", into their unambiguous equivalents, e.g., "*When was DNA discovered?*". Such unambiguous questions can be then processed by any standard QA model outside of the conversation history.

Clearly, the quality of question formulation interacts with the ability to answer this question. In this paper, we show that introducing QR component in the conversational QA architecture, by decoupling question interpretation in context from the question answering task, provides us with a unique opportunity to gain an insight on the interaction between the two tasks. Ultimately, we are interested in whether this interaction can potentially help us

[†]Work done as an intern at Apple Inc.

Proceedings of the 5th International Workshop on Search-Oriented Conversational AI (SCAI), pages 7–16
Online, November 19, 2020.

to improve the performance on the end-to-end conversational QA task. To this end we formulate our main research question:

How do differences in question formulation in a conversational setting affect question answering performance?

The standard approach to QA evaluation is to measure model performance on a benchmark dataset with respect to the ground-truth answers, such as text span overlap in the reading comprehension task, or NDCG@3 in the passage retrieval task. However, such evaluation setups may also have their limitations with respect to the biases in the task formulation and insufficient data diversity that allow models to learn shortcuts and overfit the benchmark dataset (Geirhos et al., 2020). There is already an ample evidence of the pitfalls in the evaluation setup of the reading comprehension task highlighting that the state-of-the-art models tend to learn answering questions using superficial clues (Jia and Liang, 2017; Ribeiro et al., 2018; Lewis and Fan, 2019).

We aim to further contribute to the research area studying robustness of QA models by extending the evaluation setup to the conversational QA task. To this end, we introduce an error analysis framework based on conversational question rewrites. The goal of the framework is to evaluate robustness of QA models using the inherent properties of the conversational setup itself. More specifically, we contrast the results obtained for ambiguous and rewritten questions outside of the conversation context. We show that this data is very well suited for analysing performance and debugging QA models. In our experiments, we evaluate two popular QA architectures proposed in the context of the conversational reading comprehension (QuAC) (Choi et al., 2018) and conversational passage ranking (TREC CAsT) (Dalton et al., 2019) tasks.

Our results show that the state-of-the-art models for passage retrieval are rather sensitive to differences in question formulation. On the other hand, the models trained on the reading comprehension task tend to find correct answers even to incomplete ambiguous questions. We believe that these findings can stimulate more research in this area and help to inform future evaluation setups for the conversational QA tasks.

2 Experimental Setup

To answer our research question and illustrate the application of the proposed evaluation framework in practice, we use the same experimental setup introduced in our earlier work (Vakulenko et al., 2020). This architecture consists of two independent components: QR and QA. It was previously evaluated against competitive approaches and baselines setting the new state-of-the-art results on the TREC CAsT 2019 dataset. The QR model was also shown to improve QA performance on both passage retrieval and reading comprehension tasks.

In the following subsection, we describe the datasets, models, and metrics that were used in our evaluation. Note, however, that our error analysis framework can be applied to other models and metrics as well. The only requirement for applying the framework is the QR-QA architecture that provides two separate outputs in terms of question rewrites and answers. We show that the same framework can be applied for both reading comprehension and passage retrieval tasks, although they produce different types of answers and require different evaluation metrics.

2.1 Datasets

We chose two conversational QA datasets for the evaluation of our approach: (1) TREC CAsT for conversational passage ranking (Dalton et al., 2019), and (2) CANARD, derived from Question Answering in Context (QuAC) for conversational reading comprehension (Choi et al., 2018). Since TREC CAsT is a relatively small dataset, we used only CANARD for training our QR model. The same QR model trained on CANARD was then evaluated on both CANARD and TREC CAsT independently.

Following the setup of the TREC CAsT 2019, we use the MS MARCO passage retrieval (Nguyen et al., 2016) and the TREC CAR (Dietz et al., 2018) paragraph collections. After de-duplication, the MS MARCO collection contains 8.6M documents and the TREC CAR – 29.8M documents. The model for passage retrieval is tuned on a sample from the MS MARCO passage retrieval dataset, which includes relevance judgements for 12.8M query-passage pairs with 399k unique queries (Nogueira and Cho, 2019). We evaluated on the test set with relevance judgements for 173 questions across 20 dialogues (topics).

We use CANARD (Elgohary et al., 2019) and

QuAC (Choi et al., 2018) datasets jointly to analyse performance on the reading comprehension task. CANARD is built upon the QuAC dataset by employing human annotators to rewrite original questions from QuAC dialogues into explicit questions. CANARD contains 40.5k pairs of question rewrites that can be matched to the original answers in QuAC. We use CANARD splits for training and evaluation. Each answer in QuAC is annotated with a Wikipedia passage from which it was extracted alongside the correct answer spans within this passage. We use the question rewrites provided in CANARD and passages with answer spans from QuAC. In our experiments, we refer to this joint dataset as CANARD for brevity. Our model for reading comprehension was also pre-trained using MultiQA dataset (Fisch et al., 2019) to further boost its performance. MultiQA contains 75k QA pairs from six standard QA benchmarks.

2.2 Conversational QA Architecture

Our architecture for conversational QA is designed to be modular by separating the original task into two subtasks. The subtasks are (1) QR, responsible for the conversational context understanding and question formulation, and (2) QA that exactly corresponds to the standard non-conversational task of answer selection (reading comprehension or passage retrieval). Therefore, the output of the QR component is an unambiguous question that is subsequently used as input to the QA component to produce the answer.

Question Rewriting The task of question rewriting is to reformulate every follow-up question in a conversation, such that the question can be unambiguously interpreted without accessing the conversation history. The input to the QR model is the question with previous conversation turns separated with a $[SEP]$ token (in our experiments, we use up to maximum of 5 previous conversation turns). Using our running example, the input would be: *Friedrich Miescher discovered DNA* $[SEP]$ *When?* and the expected output from the QR model is: *When was DNA discovered?*.

Our QR model is based on a unidirectional Transformer (decoder) designed for the sequence generation task. It was initialised with the weights of the pre-trained GPT2 (Radford et al., 2019) and further fine-tuned on the QR task. The training objective in QR is to predict the output sequence as in the ground truth question rewrites produced by human annotators. The model is trained via the teacher forcing approach. The loss is calculated with the negative log-likelihood (cross-entropy) function. At inference time, the question rewrites are generated recursively turn by turn for each of the dialogues using the previously generated rewrites as input corresponding to the dialogue history, i.e., previous turns.

For our experiments, we adopt the same QR model architecture proposed in the previous work (Transformer++) (Anantha et al., 2020; Vakulenko et al., 2020). It was shown to outperform a co-reference baseline and other Transformer-based models on CANARD, TREC CAsT and QReCC.

Question Answering We experiment with two different QA models that reflect the state-of-the-art in reading comprehension and passage retrieval (Nogueira and Cho, 2019). All our QA models are initialised with a pre-trained $BERT_{LARGE}$ (Devlin et al., 2019) and then fine-tuned on each of the target tasks.

Our model for reading comprehension follows the standard architecture design for this task. We restrict our implementation to the simplest but a very competitive model architecture that more complex approaches usually build upon (Liu et al., 2019; Lan et al., 2019). This model consists of a Transformer-based bidirectional encoder and an output layer that predicts the answer span. The input to the model is the sequence of tokens formed by concatenating a question and a passage, the two are separated with a $[SEP]$ token.

Our passage retrieval approach is implemented following Nogueira and Cho (2019). It uses Anserini for the candidate selection phase with BM25 (top-1000 passages) and $BERT_{LARGE}$ for the passage re-ranking phase.[1] The re-ranking model was tuned on a sample from MS MARCO with 12.8M query-passage pairs and 399k unique queries.

2.3 Metrics

We use the standard performance metrics for each of the QA subtasks. We use normalized discounted cumulative gain (*NDCG@3*) and precision on the top-passage (*P@1*) to evaluate quality of passage retrieval (with a relevance threshold of 2 in accordance with the official evaluation guidelines for CAsT). We use *F1* metric for reading comprehen-

[1] https://github.com/nyu-dl/dl4marco-bert

Table 1: Break-down analysis of the passage retrieval on TREC CAsT. Each row represents a group of QA samples that exhibit similar behaviour. We consider three types of input for every QA sample: the question from the test set (Original), generated by the best QR model (Transformer++) or rewritten manually (Human). The numbers correspond to the count of QA samples for each of the groups. The numbers in parenthesis indicate how many questions in the ground truth do not need rewriting, i.e., Human = Original.

Original	QR	Human	P@1	NDCG@3		
			= 1	> 0	≥ 0.5	= 1
×	×	×	49 (14)	10 (1)	55 (20)	154 (49)
✓	×	×	0	0	0	0
×	✓	×	2	0	1	0
✓	✓	×	0	1	1	0
×	×	✓	19	10	25	4
✓	×	✓	0	1	0	0
×	✓	✓	48	63	47	11
✓	✓	✓	55 (37)	88 (52)	44 (33)	4 (4)
			Total			173 (53)

Table 2: Break-down analysis of all reading comprehension results for the CANARD dataset, similar to Table 1. Observe that Table 1 is much more sparse than Table 2. There are almost no cases for which original or model-rewritten questions outperformed human rewriting when ranking passages. On the contrary, Table 2 indicates a considerable number of anomalous cases in which the reading comprehension model was able to answer incomplete follow-up questions but failed in answering ground-truth questions (rows 2-4).

Original	QR	Human	F1 > 0	F1 ≥ 0.5	F1 = 1
×	×	×	847 (136)	1855 (235)	2701 (332)
✓	×	×	174	193	181
×	✓	×	19	35 (2)	40 (1)
✓	✓	×	135	153	120
×	×	✓	141	288	232
✓	×	✓	65 (1)	57 (1)	40
×	✓	✓	226	324	269
✓	✓	✓	3964 (529)	2666 (428)	1988 (333)
			Total		5571 (666)

sion, which measures word overlap between the predicted answer span and the ground truth.

In contrast with QA, there is no established methodology for reporting the QR performance yet. Existing studies tend to report performance using BLEU metrics following the original CANARD paper (Yu et al., 2020; Lin et al., 2020).

We conducted a systematic evaluation of different performance metrics to find a subset that correlates with the human judgement of the quality of question rewrites (see more details in (Anantha et al., 2020)). Our analysis showed that ROUGE-1 Recall (ROUGE-1 R) (Lin, 2004) and Universal Sentence Encoder (*USE*) (Cer et al., 2018) embeddings correlate with the human judgement of the rewriting quality the most (Pearson 0.69 for ROUGE-1 R and Pearson 0.71 for USE). Therefore, we also use ROUGE-1 R and USE in this study to measure similarity between the model rewrites and the ground truth.

ROUGE is traditionally employed for evaluation of the text summarisation approaches. While ROUGE is limited to measuring lexical overlap between the two input texts, the USE model outputs dense vector representations that are designed to indicate semantic similarities between sentences beyond word overlap.

3 Our Error Analysis Framework

To trace how the difference in question formulation affects QA performance we compare the QR performance metrics with the QA performance metrics on the case-by-case basis, i.e., for each question-answer pair. Notice that we can apply the same approach for both retrieval and reading comprehension evaluation (see Table 2 for the results on reading comprehension).

Table 1 illustrates our approach. Each row of the table represents one of the combinations of the possible QA results for 3 types of question formulation. For every answer in a dataset we have 3 types of question formulation: (1) an original, possibly implicit, question (**Original**), (2) rewrites produced by the QR model (**QR**) and (3) rewrites produced by a human annotator (**Human**).

✓ indicates that the answer produced by the QA model was correct or × – incorrect, according to the thresholds provided in the right columns. For example, the first row of the table indicates the situation, when neither the original question, nor they generated or human rewrite were able to solicit the correct answer (× × ×). We then can automatically calculate how many samples in our results fall into each of these bins.

We assume human question rewrites as the ground truth. Therefore, all cases in which these rewrites did not result in a correct answer are errors of the QA component (rows 1-4 in Tables 1-2). The next two rows 5-6 show the cases, where human rewrites succeeded but the model rewrites failed, which we consider to be a likely error of the QR component. The last two rows are true positives for our model, where the last row combines cases where the original question was just copied without rewriting (numbers in brackets) and other cases

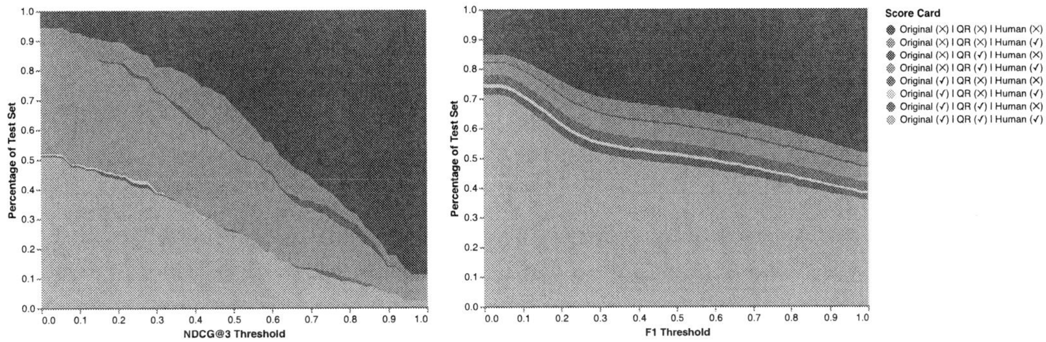

Figure 1: Break-down analysis for passage retrieval (left) and reading comprehension (right) results (best in color). This plot visualises the difference between the error distributions reported in Tables 1-2 with a sliding cut-off threshold. The blue region at the top of the plots represents the proportion of errors in QA. The orange region represents the proportion of errors in QR. The light green region shows the proportion of samples that were both rewritten and answered correctly. The pink region at the bottom shows the importance of QR for the task. The larger the region the more questions were answered correctly without any rewriting. We observe that the difference between the two plots is very pronounced. The impact of QR is noticeable in passage retrieval, which is more sensitive to question formulation than the reading comprehension model.

when rewriting was not required.

Since there is no single binary measure for the answer correctness, we can pick different cut-off thresholds for the QA metrics. For example, P@1=1 will consider the answer correct if it came up at the top of the ranking; or F1=1 will consider the answer correct only in cases with full span overlap, i.e, exact matches only. Figure 1 extends this analysis by considering all thresholds in the range [0; 1] with 0.02 intervals for NDCG@3 in retrieval and F1 in reading comprehension. This figure shows the proportion of different error types as well as the results sensitivity to the choice of the performance threshold.

4 Evaluation Results

Our approach allows us to estimate that the majority of errors stem from the QA model: 29% of the test samples for retrieval and 55% for reading comprehension. 11% of errors can be directly attributed to QR in the retrieval setup and 5% in reading comprehension.

To estimate the impact of QR on QA, we consider only the last four rows in Table 2 for which QA model return a correct answer for Human questions. Then, we divide the number of questions for which the Original question leads to the correct answer, i.e., without rewriting, by the total number of questions that can be answered correctly by our QA model (discarding the number of questions that were not rewritten by the annotators indicated in parenthesis). For example, to estimate the number of questions correctly answered in CANARD (F1 = 1) without rewriting, i.e., using the Original question as input to the QA model:

$$\frac{40 + 1988 - 333}{232 + 40 + 269 + 1988 - 333} = 0.77 \quad (1)$$

The proportion of QR errors for retrieval setup is higher than for reading comprehension setup. In particular, we found that the majority of questions in CANARD test set (77% F1 = 1) can be correctly answered using only the Original questions without any question rewriting, i.e., even when the questions are ambiguous. For TREC CAsT, the chances of reaching the correct answer set using an ambiguous question are much lower (21% P@1 = 1). See Tables 3-4 for the complete result set with different cut-off thresholds.

There are two anecdotal cases where our QR component was able to generate rewrites that helped to produce better ranking than the human-written questions. The first example shows that the re-ranking model does not handle paraphrases well. Original question: "*What are good sources in food?*", human rewrite: "*What are good sources of **melatonin** in food?*", model rewrite: "*What are good sources in food for **melatonin***". In the second example the human annotator and our model chose different context to disambiguate the original question. Original question: "*What about environmental factors?*", human rewrite: "*What about environ-*

Table 3: The fraction of questions in TREC CAsT that were answered correctly without rewriting.

Questions	P@1 = 1	NDCG@3 > 0	NDCG@3 ≥ 0.5	NDCG@3 = 1
All	0.45	0.55	0.38	0.21
Human != Original	0.21	0.34	0.13	0

Table 4: The fraction of questions in CANARD that were answered correctly without rewriting.

Questions	F1 > 0	F1 ≥ 0.5	F1 = 1
All	0.92	0.82	0.80
Human != Original	0.91	0.79	0.77

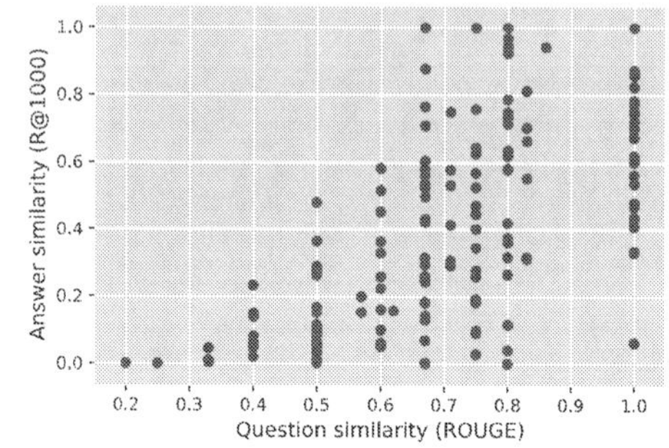

Figure 2: Strong correlation (Pearson 0.77) between question similarity (ROUGE) and the answer sets produced by the passage retrieval model (Recall).

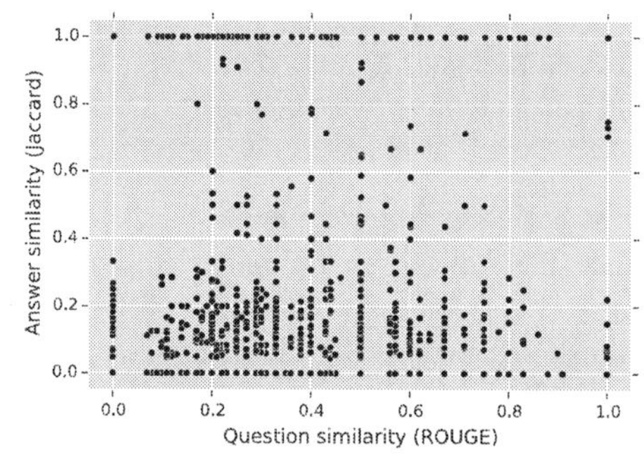

Figure 3: Weak correlation (Pearson 0.31) between question similarity (ROUGE) and answers produced by the reading comprehension model (Jaccard).

*mental factors during the **Bronze Age collapse**?*", model rewrite: "*What about environmental factors that lead to led to a **breakdown of trade***". Even though both model rewrites are not grammatically correct they solicited correct top-answers, while the human rewrites failed, which indicate flaws in the QA model performance.

5 QA-QR Correlation

In this section, we check whether the QR metrics can predict the QA performance for the individual questions by measuring the correlation between the QR and QA metrics. This analysis shows how the change in question formulation affects the answer selection. In other words, we are interested whether similar questions also produce similar answers, and whether distinct questions result in distinct answers.

To discover the correlation between question and answer similarity, we discarded all samples, where the human rewrites do not lead to the correct answers (top 4 rows in Tables 1-2). The remaining subset contains only the samples in which the QA model was able to find the correct answer. We then compute ROUGE for the pairs of human and generated rewrites, and measure its correlation with P@1 to check if rewrites similar to the correct question will also produce correct answers, and vice versa.

There is a strong correlation for ROUGE = 1, i.e., when the generated rewrite is very close to the human one. However, when ROUGE < 1 the answer is less predictable. Even for rewrites that have a relatively small lexical overlap with the ground-truth (ROUGE ≤ 0.4) it is possible to retrieve a correct answer, and vice versa.

We further explore the effect of the QR quality on the QA results by comparing differences of the answer sets produced when given different rewrites. We compare answers produced separately for human and model rewrites using the same input question. However, this time we look at all the answers produced by the QA model irrespective of whether the answers were correct or not. This setup allows us to better observe how much the change in the question formulation triggers the change in the produced answer.

Figure 2 demonstrates strong correlation between the question similarity, as measured by ROUGE, and the answer set similarity. We measured the similarity between the top-1000 answers returned for the human rewrites and the generated rewrites by computing recall (R@1000). Points in the bottom right of this plot show sensitivity of the QA component, where similar questions lead to different answer rankings. The data points that are close to the top center area indicate weaknesses of the QR metric as a proxy for the QA results: often questions do not have to be the same as the ground truth questions to solicit the same answers. The blank area in the top-left of the diagonal shows that a lexical overlap is required to produce the same answer set, which is likely due to the candidate filtering phase based on the bag-of-word representation matching.

We also compared ROUGE and Jaccard similarity for the tokens in reading comprehension results but they showed only a weak correlation (Pearson 0.31). This result confirms our observation that the extractive model tends to be rather sensitive to a slight input perturbation but will also often provide the same answer to very distinct questions.

Thus, our results show that the existing QR metrics have a limited capacity in predicting the performance on the end-to-end QA task. ROUGE correlates with the answer recall for the retrieval model, but cannot be used to reliably predict answer correctness for the individual question rewrites. Since ROUGE treats all the tokens equally (except for the stop-word list) it is unable to capture importance of the individual tokens that modify question semantics. The correlation of the QA performance with the embedding-based USE metric is even lower than with ROUGE for the both QA models.

6 Discussion

We showed that QA results can identify question paraphrases. However, this property directly depends on the ability of the QA model to match equivalent questions to the same answer set.

Wrong answer or wrong question? Our passage retrieval model is using BM25 as a filtering step, which relies on the lexical match between the terms in the question and the terms in the passage. Hence, synonyms, like "large" and "big", cannot be matched with this model. This effect explains that dissimilar questions are never matched to the same answers in Figure 2. The drawback of this model is that it suffers from the "vocabulary mismatch" problem (Van Gysel, 2017).

A one-word difference between a pair of questions may have a very little as well as a very dramatic effect on the question interpretation. This class of errors corresponds to the variance evident from Figure 2.

Our error analysis indicates that small perturbations of the input question, such as anaphora resolution, often cause a considerable change in the answer ranking. For example, the pair of the original question: "*Who are the Hamilton Electors and what were **they** trying to do?*", and the human rewrite: "*Who are the Hamilton Electors and what were the **Hamilton Electors** trying to do?*" produce ROUGE = 1 but R@1000 = 0.33. We also identified many cases in which inability of the QR component to generate apostrophes resulted in incorrect answers (original question: "*Describe **Netflixs** subscriber growth over time*", and the human rewrite: "*Describe **Netflix's** subscriber growth over time*").

In contrast, our reading comprehension models is based solely on the dense vector representations, which should be able to deal with paraphrases. In practice, we see from Figure 3 that this feature may also introduce an important drawback, when the model produces a correct answer even when given an incorrectly formulated question. This stability and undersensitivity of the reading comprehension model may indicate biases in the dataset and evaluation setup. When the answers no longer depends on the question being asked, but can be also predicted independently from the question, the QA model evidently fails to learn the mechanisms underlying QA. Instead, it may learn a shortcut in the benchmark dataset that allows to guess correct questions, such as likely answer positioning within an article.

Our experiments show that the retrieval-based setup is more adequate in judging model robustness. The size of the answer space is sufficiently large so as to exclude spurious cues that the model can exploit for shortcut learning. The role of QR is, therefore, much more evident in this task, since to be able to find the correct answer the question has to be formulated well by disambiguating conversational context. While it may be redundant to overspecify the question when given several passages to choose the answer from, it becomes of a vital importance when given several million passages. This argument holds, however, only when assuming a uniform answer distribution, which is often not the case unless for sufficiently large web collections. This particular observation brings us to the next question that we would like to discuss in more detail.

Rewrite or not to rewrite? Our experiments demonstrated the challenges in the quality control of the QR task itself. Human rewrites are not perfect themselves since it is not always clear whether and what should be rewritten. Considering the human judgment of the QR quality independent from the QA results, little deviations may not seem important. However, from the pragmatic point of view, they may have a major impact on the overall performance of the end-to-end system.

The level of detail required to answer a particular question is often not apparent and depends on the dataset. However, we can argue that inconsistencies, such as typos and paraphrases, should be handled by the QA component, since they do not originate from the context interpretation errors.

Further on, we evaluated our assumption about human rewrites as the reliable ground truth. Our evaluation results indeed showed that human rewriting was redundant in certain cases. There are cases in which original questions without rewriting were already sufficient to retrieve the correct answers from the passage collection (see last row of the Table 1). In particular, we found that 10% of the questions in TREC CAsT were rewritten by human annotators that did not need rewriting to retrieve the correct answer. For example, original question: "*What is the functionalist theory?*", human rewrite: "*What is the functionalist theory in **sociology**?*". However, in another question from the same dialogue, omitting the same word from the rewrite leads to retrieval of an irrelevant passage, since there are multiple alternative answers.

The need for QR essentially interacts with the size and diversity of the possible answer space, e.g., collection content, with respect to the question. Some of the questions were correctly answered even with underspecified questions, e.g., original question: "*What are some ways to avoid injury?*", human rewrite: "*What are some ways to avoid **sports** injuries?*", because of the collection bias.

The goal of QR is to learn patterns that correct question formulation independent from the collection content. This approach is similar to how humans handle this task when formulating search queries, i.e., based on their knowledge of language and the world. Humans can spot ambiguity regardless of the information source by modeling the expected content of the information source even without the need to have direct access to it. Clearly, this expectation may not be optimal or even sufficient to be able to formulate a single precise question, which is exactly the point at which the need for an information-seeking dialogue naturally arises.

When the question formulation procedure is designed to be independent of the collection content, it also allows for querying several sources with the same question. This property is especially helpful when the content of the collection is unknown, which also allows to work with 3rd party APIs to access information in a distributed fashion. We may see a similar effect as in human-human communication here as well, when the need for an automated information-seeking dialogue between distributed systems may arise to better negotiate the information need and disambiguate the question further with respect to the content of each remote information source.

7 Related Work

Several recent research studies reported that state-of-the-art machine learning models lack in robustness across several NLP tasks (Li and Specia, 2019; Zeng et al., 2019). In particular, these models were found to be sensitive to input perturbations.

Jia and Liang (2017) analysed this problem in the context of the reading comprehension task. They showed in the experimental evaluation that QA models suffer from overstability, i.e., they tend to provide the same answer to a different question, when it is sufficiently similar to the correct question. Lewis and Fan (2019) also showed this deficiency of the state-of-the-art models for reading comprehension that learn to attend to just a few words in the question.

Our evaluation results support these findings using the conversational settings. We showed that many ambiguous questions in QuAC can be answered correctly without the conversation history (see Table 2). In contrast, this effect is absent in the passage retrieval setup (see Table 1 or Figure 1). These results suggest that the passage retrieval evaluation setup is more adequate for training robust QA models.

Previous work that focused on analysing and explaining performance of Transformer-based models on the ranking task used word attention visualisation and random removals of non-stop words (Dai and Callan, 2019; Qiao et al., 2019). The analysis framework proposed here provides a more systematic approach to model evaluation using ambiguous and rewritten question pairs, which is a by-product of applying QR in conversational QA.

Our approach is most similar to the one proposed by Ribeiro et al. (2018), who used semantically equivalent adversaries to analyse performance in several NLP tasks, including reading comprehension, visual QA and sentiment analysis. Similarly, in our approach, question rewrites, as paraphrases with different levels of ambiguity, are a natural choice for evaluation of the conversational QA performance. The difference is that we do not need to generate semantically equivalent questions but can reuse question rewrites as a by-product of introducing the QR model as a component of the conversational QA architecture.

8 Conclusion

QR is a challenging but a very insightful task designed to capture linguistic patterns that identify and resolve ambiguity in question formulation. Our results demonstrate the utility of QR as not only enabler for conversational QA but also as a tool that helps to understand when QA models fail.

We introduced an effective error analysis framework for conversational QA using QR and used it to evaluate sensitivity of two state-of-the-art QA model architectures (for reading comprehension and passage retrieval tasks). Moreover, the framework we introduced is agnostic to the model architecture and can be reused for performance evaluation of different models using other evaluation metrics as well.

QR helps to analyse model performance and discover their weaknesses, such as oversensitivity and undersensitivity to differences in question formulation. In particular, the reading comprehension task setup is inadequate to reflect the real performance of a question interpretation component since ambiguous or even incorrect question formulations are likely to result in a correct answer span. In passage retrieval, we observe an opposite effect. Since the space of possible answers is very large it is impossible to hit the correct answer by chance. We discover, however, that these models tend to suffer from oversensitivity instead, i.e., when even a single character will trigger a considerable change in answer ranking.

In future work, we should extend our evaluation to dense passage retrieval models and examine their performance using the conversational QA setup with the QR model. We should also look into training approaches that could allow QA models to further benefit from the QR component. As we showed in our experiments QR provides useful intermediate outputs that can be interpreted by humans and used for evaluation. We believe that QR models can be also useful for training more robust QA models. Both components can be trained jointly, which is inline with Lewis and Fan (2019), who showed that the joint objective of question and answer generation further improves QA performance.

Acknowledgements

We would like to thank our colleagues Srinivas Chappidi, Bjorn Hoffmeister, Stephan Peitz, Russ Webb, Drew Frank, and Chris DuBois for their insightful comments.

References

Raviteja Anantha, Svitlana Vakulenko, Zhucheng Tu, Shayne Longpre, Stephen Pulman, and Srinivas Chappidi. 2020. Open-Domain Question Answering Goes Conversational via Question Rewriting. *arXiv preprint*.

Daniel Cer, Yinfei Yang, Sheng-yi Kong, Nan Hua, Nicole Limtiaco, Rhomni St. John, Noah Constant, Mario Guajardo-Cespedes, Steve Yuan, Chris Tar, Brian Strope, and Ray Kurzweil. 2018. Universal Sentence Encoder for English. In *Proceedings of the 2018 Conference on Empirical Methods in Natural Language Processing*. 169–174.

Eunsol Choi, He He, Mohit Iyyer, Mark Yatskar, Wen-tau Yih, Yejin Choi, Percy Liang, and Luke Zettlemoyer. 2018. QuAC: Question Answering in Context. In *Proceedings of the 2018 Conference on Empirical Methods in Natural Language Processing*. 2174–2184.

Zhuyun Dai and Jamie Callan. 2019. Deeper text understanding for IR with contextual neural language modeling. In *Proceedings of the 42nd International ACM SIGIR Conference on Research and Development in Information Retrieval*. 985–988.

Jeffrey Dalton, Chenyan Xiong, and Jamie Callan. 2019. CAsT 2019: The Conversational Assistance Track Overview. In *Proceedings of the 28th Text REtrieval Conference*. 13–15.

Jacob Devlin, Ming-Wei Chang, Kenton Lee, and Kristina Toutanova. 2019. BERT: Pre-training of Deep Bidirectional Transformers for Language Understanding. In *Proceedings of the 2019 Conference of the North American Chapter of the Association for Computational Linguistics: Human Language Technologies*. 4171–4186.

Laura Dietz, Ben Gamari, Jeff Dalton, and Nick Craswell. 2018. TREC Complex Answer Retrieval Overview. TREC.

Ahmed Elgohary, Denis Peskov, and Jordan Boyd-Graber. 2019. Can You Unpack That? Learning to Rewrite Questions-in-Context. In *Proceedings of the*

2019 Conference on Empirical Methods in Natural Language Processing and the 9th International Joint Conference on Natural Language Processing. 5920–5926.

Adam Fisch, Alon Talmor, Robin Jia, Minjoon Seo, Eunsol Choi, and Danqi Chen. 2019. MRQA 2019 Shared Task: Evaluating Generalization in Reading Comprehension. *arXiv preprint arXiv:1910.09753* (2019).

Robert Geirhos, Jörn-Henrik Jacobsen, Claudio Michaelis, Richard S. Zemel, Wieland Brendel, Matthias Bethge, and Felix A. Wichmann. 2020. Shortcut Learning in Deep Neural Networks. *CoRR* abs/2004.07780 (2020).

Yunlong He, Jiliang Tang, Hua Ouyang, Changsung Kang, Dawei Yin, and Yi Chang. 2016. Learning to rewrite queries. In *Proceedings of the 25th ACM International on Conference on Information and Knowledge Management*. 1443–1452.

Robin Jia and Percy Liang. 2017. Adversarial Examples for Evaluating Reading Comprehension Systems. In *Proceedings of the 2017 Conference on Empirical Methods in Natural Language Processing, EMNLP 2017, Copenhagen, Denmark, September 9-11, 2017*. 2021–2031.

Zhenzhong Lan, Mingda Chen, Sebastian Goodman, Kevin Gimpel, Piyush Sharma, and Radu Soricut. 2019. Albert: A lite BERT for self-supervised learning of language representations. *arXiv preprint arXiv:1909.11942* (2019).

Mike Lewis and Angela Fan. 2019. Generative Question Answering: Learning to Answer the Whole Question. In *7th International Conference on Learning Representations, ICLR 2019, New Orleans, LA, USA, May 6-9, 2019*.

Zhenhao Li and Lucia Specia. 2019. Improving Neural Machine Translation Robustness via Data Augmentation: Beyond Back-Translation. In *Proceedings of the 5th Workshop on Noisy User-generated Text, W-NUT@EMNLP 2019, Hong Kong, China, November 4, 2019*. 328–336.

Chin-Yew Lin. 2004. Rouge: A package for automatic evaluation of summaries. In *Text summarization branches out*. 74–81.

Sheng-Chieh Lin, Jheng-Hong Yang, Rodrigo Nogueira, Ming-Feng Tsai, Chuan-Ju Wang, and Jimmy Lin. 2020. Query Reformulation using Query History for Passage Retrieval in Conversational Search. *arXiv preprint arXiv:2005.02230* (2020).

Yinhan Liu, Myle Ott, Naman Goyal, Jingfei Du, Mandar Joshi, Danqi Chen, Omer Levy, Mike Lewis, Luke Zettlemoyer, and Veselin Stoyanov. 2019. Roberta: A robustly optimized bert pretraining approach. *arXiv preprint arXiv:1907.11692* (2019).

Tri Nguyen, Mir Rosenberg, Xia Song, Jianfeng Gao, Saurabh Tiwary, Rangan Majumder, and Li Deng. 2016. MS MARCO: A Human Generated MAchine Reading COmprehension Dataset. In *Proceedings of the Workshop on Cognitive Computation: Integrating neural and symbolic approaches*.

Rodrigo Nogueira and Kyunghyun Cho. 2019. Passage Re-ranking with BERT. *arXiv preprint arXiv:1901.04085* (2019).

Yifan Qiao, Chenyan Xiong, Zhenghao Liu, and Zhiyuan Liu. 2019. Understanding the Behaviors of BERT in Ranking. *arXiv preprint arXiv:1904.07531* (2019).

Alec Radford, Jeffrey Wu, Rewon Child, David Luan, Dario Amodei, and Ilya Sutskever. 2019. Language models are unsupervised multitask learners. *OpenAI Blog* 1, 8 (2019).

Siva Reddy, Danqi Chen, and Christopher D Manning. 2019. CoQA: A Conversational Question Answering Challenge. *Transactions of the Association for Computational Linguistics* 7 (2019), 249–266.

Gary Ren, Xiaochuan Ni, Manish Malik, and Qifa Ke. 2018. Conversational query understanding using sequence to sequence modeling. In *Proceedings of the 2018 World Wide Web Conference*. 1715–1724.

Marco Túlio Ribeiro, Sameer Singh, and Carlos Guestrin. 2018. Semantically Equivalent Adversarial Rules for Debugging NLP models. In *Proceedings of the 56th Annual Meeting of the Association for Computational Linguistics, ACL 2018, Melbourne, Australia, July 15-20, 2018, Volume 1: Long Papers*. 856–865.

Svitlana Vakulenko, Shayne Longpre, Zhucheng Tu, and Raviteja Anantha. 2020. Question Rewriting for Conversational Question Answering. *arXiv preprint arXiv:2004.14652*.

Christophe Van Gysel. 2017. *Remedies against the vocabulary gap in information retrieval*. Ph.D. Dissertation. University of Amsterdam.

Shi Yu, Jiahua Liu, Jingqin Yang, Chenyan Xiong, Paul Bennett, Jianfeng Gao, and Zhiyuan Liu. 2020. Few-Shot Generative Conversational Query Rewriting. In *Proceedings of the 43rd International ACM SIGIR conference on research and development in Information Retrieval, SIGIR 2020, Virtual Event, China, July 25-30, 2020*. 1933–1936.

Xiaohui Zeng, Chenxi Liu, Yu-Siang Wang, Weichao Qiu, Lingxi Xie, Yu-Wing Tai, Chi-Keung Tang, and Alan L. Yuille. 2019. Adversarial Attacks Beyond the Image Space. In *IEEE Conference on Computer Vision and Pattern Recognition, CVPR 2019, Long Beach, CA, USA, June 16-20, 2019*. 4302–4311.

Multi-Task Learning using Dynamic Task Weighting for Conversational Question Answering

Sarawoot Kongyoung
University of Glasgow
s.kongyoung.1@research.gla.ac.uk

Craig Macdonald, Iadh Ounis
University of Glasgow
{*first.lastname*}@glasgow.ac.uk

Abstract

Conversational Question Answering (ConvQA) is a Conversational Search task in a simplified setting, where an answer must be extracted from a given passage. Neural language models, such as BERT, fine-tuned on large-scale ConvQA datasets such as CoQA and QuAC have been used to address this task. Recently, Multi-Task Learning (MTL) has emerged as a particularly interesting approach for developing ConvQA models, where the objective is to enhance the performance of a primary task by sharing the learned structure across several related *auxiliary* tasks. However, existing ConvQA models that leverage MTL have not investigated the *dynamic* adjustment of the relative importance of the different tasks during learning, nor the resulting impact on the performance of the learned models. In this paper, we first study the effectiveness and efficiency of dynamic MTL methods including Evolving Weighting, Uncertainty Weighting, and Loss-Balanced Task Weighting, compared to *static* MTL methods such as the uniform weighting of tasks. Furthermore, we propose a novel hybrid dynamic method combining Abridged Linear for the main task with a Loss-Balanced Task Weighting (LBTW) for the auxiliary tasks, so as to automatically fine-tune task weighting during learning, ensuring that each of the tasks' weights is adjusted by the relative importance of the different tasks. We conduct experiments using QuAC, a large-scale ConvQA dataset. Our results demonstrate the effectiveness of our proposed method, which significantly outperforms both the single-task learning and static task weighting methods with improvements ranging from +2.72% to +3.20% in F1 scores. Finally, our findings show that the performance of using MTL in developing ConvQA model is sensitive to the correct selection of the auxiliary tasks as well as to an adequate balancing of the loss rates of these tasks during training by using LBTW.

1 Introduction

The task of Conversational Question Answering (ConvQA), which consists in answering a question from a given passage in the form of a dialogue has become a vital task for Machine Reading Comprehension (MRC). In the ConvQA task, in order to predict an answer, the system needs to extract text spans from a given passage and understand the question based on the given conversational history. Recently, the advancement in neural language modeling such as BERT (Devlin et al., 2019), and the introduction of two large-scale datasets, namely CoQA (Reddy et al., 2019) and QuAC (Choi et al., 2018) have further boosted research in the ConvQA task. In particular, QuAC introduces a main task, namely Answer Span prediction, which consists in answering a question by extracting text spans from a given passage as well as some *auxiliary* tasks, namely Yes/No prediction, Follow up prediction and Unanswerable prediction. Recently, Multi-Task Learning (MTL), which is a way to learn multiple different but related tasks simultaneously, has emerged as a popular solution to tackle all these tasks in a uniform model (Qu et al., 2019b). MTL can also be used to leverage the auxiliary tasks to improve the performance of a system on the main task. For example, for the QuAC dataset, (Qu et al., 2019b; Yeh and Chen, 2019) adopted an MTL approach that learns the *auxiliary* tasks and the main task by sharing the encoder, and showed an improvement in the used ConvQA model.

MTL methods can be categorised into static or dynamic methods. In the static MTL methods, each of the task's weights used to combine the loss functions of the various used tasks during training are unchanged throughout the learning phase, which may divert training resources to unnecessary tasks. In contrast, in the dynamic MTL methods, each of the task's weights are adjusted automatically

Proceedings of the 5th International Workshop on Search-Oriented Conversational AI (SCAI), pages 17–26
Online, November 19, 2020.

to balance the loss rate (Liu et al., 2019a) or to balance the weights across tasks (Kendall et al.). However, the implementation of a MTL dynamic method is more complicated and has a lower training efficiency than static methods.

Most existing (Qu et al., 2019b; Yeh and Chen, 2019) Conversational Question Answering (ConvQA) models that leverage Multi-Task Learning (MTL) use the static method with unchanged tasks' weights during the training epochs. For instance, the recently-proposed History Attention Mechanism (HAM) model (Qu et al., 2019b) attempted to apply Multi-Task Learning in order to improve the effectiveness of conversational QA. However, the tasks' weights in the model were unchanged during the training state and emphasise the main task. FlowDelta (Yeh and Chen, 2019) is a ConvQA model that also employed a static MTL method, which sets all tasks' weights equal to one. In the static MTL methods used in HAM and FlowDelta, all of the tasks' weights have not been adjusted throughout the learning phase. As a result, training resources could be diverted to unnecessary tasks with a negative impact on the performance of the learned models. To improve the effectiveness of Multi-Task Learning for Conversational Question Answering, we propose a novel method, called Hybrid Task Weighting, which focuses on adjusting the tasks' weights by modelling the difference between the tasks' weights, while still prioritising on the main task.

Our contributions are summarised as follows: (1) We leverage dynamic Multi-Task Learning with BERT[1] to effectively address the task of learning Answer Span prediction with its auxiliary tasks including Yes/No prediction, Follow up prediction, and Unanswerable prediction; (2) To further enhance the performance of Multi-Task Learning, we introduce a hybrid strategy, which automatically fine-tunes the multiple tasks' weights along the learning steps. Our method uses Abridged Linear for the primary task and Loss-Balanced Task Weighting for the auxiliary tasks; (3) The proposed hybrid method yields the best performance improvements over the baselines on the QuAC dataset.

2 Related Work

In the following, we discuss related work about Multi-Task Learning, Conversational Question Answering, and using Multi-Task Learning in Conversational Question Answering.

[1] Our preliminary experiments found BERT to be more effective than ALBERT or RoBERTa.

Multi-Task Learning: MTL is a learning paradigm, which has achieved success in many machine learning applications, including Natural Language Processing (Liu et al., 2015, 2019b), Speech Processing (Hu et al., 2015; Wu et al., 2015), and Computer Vision (Leang et al., 2020). For further background on MTL, we refer the readers to the recent review by (Ruder, 2017; Zhang and Yang, 2017). The MTL methods can be classified into static methods or dynamic methods based on their weighting strategy (Ming et al., 2019). In a static method, before training the network, each of the task's weights is set manually, then these weights are fixed throughout the training of the network (Qu et al., 2019b; Yeh and Chen, 2019). In contrast, the dynamic methods initialise each of the task's weights at the beginning of the training and automatically update the weights during the training process (Belharbi et al., 2016; Chen et al., 2018; Liu et al., 2019a). Typically, the MTL networks can be classified into either *hard* or *soft* parameter sharing networks (Ruder, 2017). In hard parameter sharing, also known as multi-head, the network is applied by employing separate task-specific output layers on top of a shared encoder. In soft parameter sharing, all parameters are task-specific but all networks have mechanisms to handle the cross-task learning. Following (Liu et al., 2015, 2019b; Xu et al., 2019), we employ a hard parameter sharing MTL approach because this network type reduces the risk of overfitting (Ruder, 2017).

Conversational Question Answering: ConvQA is a Machine Reading Comprehension (MRC) task where questions are formed in conversations. Hence, a ConvQA approach needs to deal with the conversation history to accurately understand and answer the current question. To handle the conversation history, existing works (Zhu et al., 2018; Reddy et al., 2019) prepended previous questions and answers to the current question while (Qu et al., 2019a,b; Yeh and Chen, 2019) employed a history selection mechanism. Some prior studies have integrated the conversation history into neural language models such as BERT: For example, Qu et al. (2019b) proposed the Positional History Answer Embedding (PosHAE) approach, which uses a feature vector to encode the position of the answer in the conversation history in the current question; Similarly, Choi et al. (2018); Yeh and Chen (2019) used a Context Feature to mark historical answers in the passage.

The two recent large-scale ConvQA datasets, QuAC (Choi et al., 2018) and CoQA (Reddy et al., 2019), have facilitated further research on this task. The differences between these datasets are that the questions in CoQA are predominantly factoid in nature, while most questions in QuAC are non-factoid. Moreover, QuAC also contains three auxiliary tasks; in contrast, CoQA only provides an Unanswerable prediction task as an auxiliary task. Hence, due to the presence of multiple auxiliary tasks, our MTL study focuses on the QuAC dataset.

Multi-Task Learning for Conversational Question Answering Models: Recently, existing works (Qu et al., 2019b; Yeh and Chen, 2019) on MTL for ConvQA have successfully adopted static MTL methods. However, there is still room for improvement since during the learning phase the weights for the auxiliary tasks are unchanged and therefore they not adjusted relative to the importance of the different tasks. We include these MTL methods as baselines in our present work.

Instead, in this paper, we take advantage of a dynamic method in MTL for ConvQA. The goal of our proposed model is to improve the effectiveness of the ConvQA task. As far we know, no prior work has addressed the use of dynamic MTL methods for the ConvQA task. In our proposed MTL approach, we employ the Abridged Linear (Belharbi et al., 2016) for the primary task and the Loss-Balanced Task Weighting (Liu et al., 2019a) for the auxiliary tasks, which prioritises the primary task after step t during training by setting the task's weight to one while also automatically fine-tuning the tasks' weights by balancing the loss ratio of the auxiliary tasks. In our model, we employ BERT (Devlin et al., 2019), which is still a widely used and popular pre-trained model, with customised features following (Qu et al., 2019b; Yeh and Chen, 2019). In the following section, we describe in detail our ConvQA model.

3 The BERT ConvQA Model

We first define the task in Section 3.1. An overview of the proposed ConvQA model is provided in Section 3.2. Section 3.3 describes how additional features are integrated with the BERT encoder. Then we explain how predictions are made for the main Answer Span prediction task as well as the auxiliary tasks in Sections 3.4 & 3.5, respectively.

Table 1: An example dialog from the ConvQA dataset.

p	In 1934 he batted .344 with 18 home runs, 104 RBI, 102 runs scored and 192 hits in 138 games. After a disappointing final season with the White Sox which saw Simmons bat just .267 with 16 home runs and 79 RBI in 128 game (first time in his 11-year career he did not reach .300+ & 100 RBI) he rebounded by hitting .327 with 13 home runs, 112 RBI and 96 runs scored in 1936 for the Detroit Tigers. In 1937 he struggled again, this time with the Washington Senators, batting just .279 with 8 home runs and 84 RBIs in 103 games. He rebounded with a stellar season in 1938, batting .302 with 21 home runs and 95 RBI in just 125 games for Washington. His 21 home runs that year gave Simmons the distinction of being the first player to hit 20 home runs in a year for the Senators. CANNOTANSWER
q_1	Where was he playing in 1933?
a_1	CANNOTANSWER
q_2	What did he do between 1933 and 1938?
a_2	In 1934 he batted .344 with 18 home runs, 104 RBI, 102 runs scored and 192 hits in 138 games.
q_3	Did he lead the league in hitting?
a_3	After a disappointing final season with the White Sox

3.1 Task Definition

Following Choi et al. (2018), we describe the ConvQA task as follows: given a passage p, a conversation history H_k consisting of a list of k questions and ground truth answer pairs, i.e. $H_k = [\langle q, a \rangle]$, and a new query q_{k+1}, the task is to predict answer a_{k+1} by predicting answer span indices i, j within passage p. Table 1 exemplifies the ConvQA task, showing an example passage p, and a history of length $k = 2$ with corresponding questions and answers; In particular, in response to question q_3, the aim of a ConvQA system is to correctly predict the right answer a_3 from all possible sentences in p.

Moreover, as mentioned in Section 2, the QuAC dataset (Choi et al., 2018) provides labels for auxiliary tasks that are relevant to the ConvQA task, namely the affirmation (Yes/No) and continuation (Follow up) classification tasks. For example, Yeh and Chen (2019) showed how to leverage the unanswerable questions as another auxiliary task called Unanswerable prediction. In the next section, we provide an overview of a BERT-based model that can be used for the ConvQA task; Moreover as an MTL model, it can benefit from learning using the auxiliary tasks. Later, in Section 4, we describe different MTL methods for weighting the ConvQA and auxiliary tasks during learning, which we apply and evaluate. We describe all auxiliary tasks in detail in Section 6.1.

3.2 Model Overview

To tackle the tasks described in Section 3.1, we present our ConvQA model by adopting a Multi-Task Learning approach. Figure 1 illustrates the architecture of our model, which consists of three components: an encoder, an answer span predictor and the auxiliary tasks predictor. For the encoder, we deploy a BERT model that encodes the question q_{k+1}, the passage p, and the conversation history H_k as a sequence of m words $C = \{c1, c2, ..., cm\}$

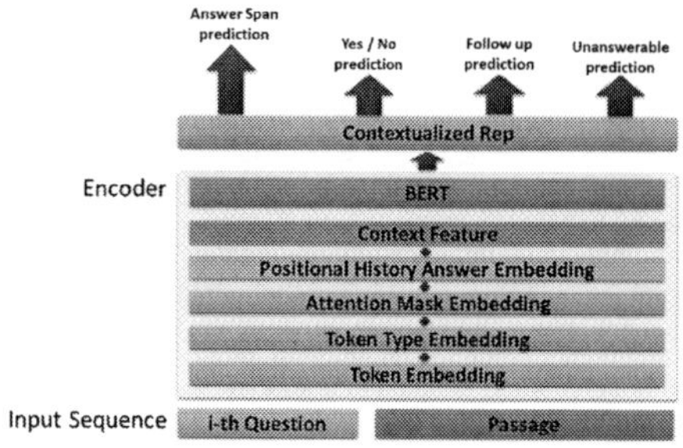

Figure 1: The model architecture.

into contextualised token-level representations i.e., $\hat{T}_k = F(q_{k+1}, p, H_k)$, where $F(\cdot)$ is BERT's encoder transformation function. These encodings are customised to the task by integrating conversation history features (Section 3.3). Finally, these representations are fed into the predictors' modules in a Multi-Task Learning setting (Sections 3.4 & 3.5).

3.3 BERT Encoder Features

In our model, we modify the BERT input to encapsulate two features – the Positional History Answer Embedding (PosHAE) and the Context Features:

PosHAE: We use this modification feature introduced by Qu et al. (2019b) to capture the conversation history into BERT. As exemplified by the example in Table 1, questions in the QuAC dataset often refer to entities in the previous answer(s). Consequently, PosHAE was introduced to embed the relative position of the terms that occur in previous answers within the conversational history H_k.

Context Feature: We integrate contextual knowledge of the previous answer within the passage into BERT by following Yeh and Chen (2019) who, applied BiDAF++ (Choi et al., 2018). Indeed, BiDAF++ learns a passage embedding that denotes whether a token in a recent answer is part of passage p.

3.4 Answer Span prediction

Given the token-level representation $\hat{T}_k$ produced by BERT, we compute the probability of each token being the start token or the end token in order to predict the answer span. In particular, to map a token representation $\hat{T}_k$ to a logit, two sets of parameters are learned for the start vector and the end vector, respectively. After that the softmax function is applied to obtain probabilities across all tokens in the sequence C (see Section 3.2). From this, we obtain p^S_m, and p^E_m, which are the probabilities of token m being the start token or end token, as follows:

$$p^S_m = \text{softmax}(\hat{T}_k(m)), p^E_m = \text{softmax}(\hat{T}_k(m)). \quad (1)$$

Then for the Answer Span prediction task, we compute the cross-entropy loss as follows:

$$\mathcal{L}_S = -\sum_M \mathbb{1}\{m = m_S\} \log(p^S_m),$$
$$\mathcal{L}_E = -\sum_M \mathbb{1}\{m = m_E\} \log(p^E_m),$$
$$\mathcal{L}_{ans} = \frac{1}{2}(\mathcal{L}_S + \mathcal{L}_E) \quad (2)$$

where the ground truth of the start token and end token are m_S and m_E, respectively, and $\mathbb{1}\{\cdot\}$ is and indicator function to show that the predicted token m is in the ground truth. Then the loss of the Answer Span prediction $\mathcal{L}_{ans}$ is calculated by averaging the loss of the start and end tokens, $\mathcal{L}_S$ and $\mathcal{L}_E$.

3.5 Auxiliary Task Prediction

All auxiliary tasks in our datasets are formulated as binary or multi-label classification tasks. To address each auxiliary task, we take the sequence-level representation $\hat{s}_k$ that is obtained from the $[CLS]$ token (which is the first token of the sequence, produced by BERT). We apply a softmax function on $\hat{s}_k$ to compute the posterior probabilities across the true and false labels for the multi-label tasks; for the binary tasks, we use a sigmoid function. After that, we compute cross-entropy loss for the multi-label tasks and the binary cross-entropy loss functions for the binary tasks. Next, we describe the MTL approaches to combine the loss functions from the auxiliary tasks with the loss calculated on the main task.

4 Multi-Task Learning for ConvQA

We now describe and categorise existing loss weighting approaches as either *static* or *dynamic*, depending on whether the importance they place on the loss of each task during learning is fixed or varied. In the following, we describe existing static and dynamic approaches (Sections 4.1 & 4.2), before describing our hybrid approach (Section 4.3).

4.1 Static MTL

Static MTL methods, which are the most frequently used MTL approaches for ConvQA, apply a fixed weighting of the different loss functions of the auxiliary tasks throughout the training process. This

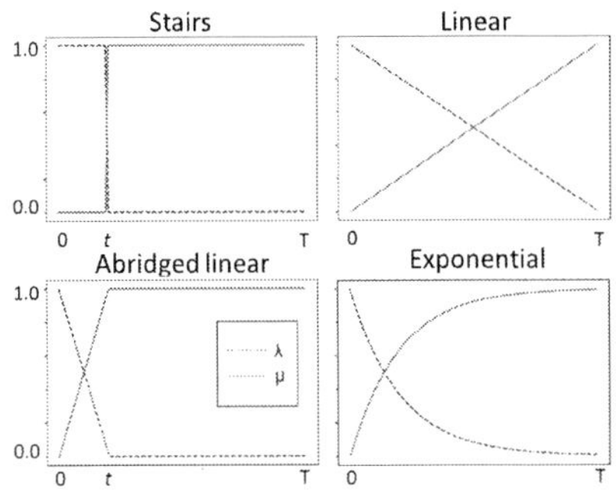

Figure 2: Dynamic Evolving Weighting approaches.

strategy is simple but yet expensive to fine-tune. Instead, many previous studies just report the use of uniform weights for tasks, such as setting all of them to 1.0 (Yeh and Chen, 2019), or setting their sum to 1 (Qu et al., 2019b). The total loss function of this method is defined as follows:

$$\mathcal{L}_{total} = \mu\mathcal{L}_{ans} + \lambda \sum_{a \in A} \mathcal{L}_a \tag{3}$$

where A is the set of auxiliary tasks, μ is the weight for the main task and λ is the weight for A.

4.2 Dynamic MTL

Applying static weighting to the auxiliary tasks can unnecessarily apply learning resources to the auxiliary tasks, instead of the main task. Indeed, this can lead to an overfitting to the wrong task and hence to underfitting on the main task (Chen et al., 2018). On the other hand, in the dynamic MTL approaches, the loss weighting of the tasks is instead continually adjusted during learning. Examples of dynamic approaches are Evolving Weighting (Belharbi et al., 2016), Loss-Balanced Task Weighting (Liu et al., 2019a), and Uncertainty Weighting (Kendall et al.), discussed further below.

Evolving Weighting: Belharbi et al. (2016) proposed to evolve the loss weighting during the training steps according to a *schedule*. A training step is defined as the number of batches of the training data, such that the total number of steps is the number of batches multiplied by the number of training epochs. Four different schedules were proposed. Figure 2 gives an overview of how the four schedules vary the weights of the main and auxiliary tasks – μ and λ, respectively – across the training steps. These four schedules are described below:

Stairs schedule: The initial emphasis is on the auxiliary task, with $\mu = 0$ and $\lambda = 1$. At a given training step t, $\mu = 1$ and $\lambda = 0$.

Algorithm 1: Hybrid Task Weighting

Given S tasks and parameter α.
Initialise neural network weights W.
for each epoch i **do**
  for each batch of data B **do**
    Get the loss on each task $\ell_B \in \mathbb{R}^S$
    Store the first batch loss as $\ell_{(0,i)} \in \mathbb{R}^S$
    if step $t \leq t_\tau$
      Set the main task weight $\mu = (\frac{t}{T})$
    else
      Set the main task weight $\mu = 1$
    for each auxiliary task s **do**
      Set the auxiliary task weight $\lambda = (\frac{\ell_{(B,s)}}{\ell_{(0,i,s)}})^\alpha$
      Update weighted loss $\ell_{(B,s)} = \ell_{(B,s)} \times \lambda$
    Update weighted loss $\ell_{(B,m)} = \ell_{(B,m)} \times \mu$
    Set the total loss $\ell_{total} = \ell_{(B,m)} + \sum_{i=1}^{s} \ell_i$

Linear schedule: The weight of the auxiliary task decreases linearly at each training step, such that the auxiliary weight $\lambda = 1$ tends to 0; in contrast, the weight of the main task increases linearly, i.e. $\lambda = (1 - \mu)$. In particular, given that the total number of steps T is known in advance, $\lambda_t = \frac{t}{\mathrm{T}}$.

Abridged Linear schedule: In a linear schedule, μ rises over the full training schedule to step T. This may not place sufficient emphasis on the main task during training. Instead, in the Abridged Linear schedule the weight on the auxiliary task λ falls linearly to 0 by a threshold step t_τ. After t_τ, all emphasis is on the main task (i.e. $\mu = 1$).

Exponential schedule: The weights evolve exponentially to the step number, i.e. $\mu = exp(\frac{-t}{\sigma})$, where t is the current number of training steps, and σ is the slope, as shown in Figure 2.

Loss-Balanced Task Weighting (LBTW) (Liu et al., 2019a): This MTL method aims to reduce *negative transfer* by using the task-specific loss to balance the different auxiliary tasks. Negative transfer is when the performance of the task is decreased by Multi-Task Learning compared to the single-task learning. This method employs the *loss ratio* between the current loss and the initial loss of each task to adjust the task's weight. The task with the loss ratio closest to one needs to contribute more to the total loss. By increasing the weight of the task with loss ratio that is closest to one, this method attempts to *balance* the task importances.

Uncertainty Weighting (Kendall et al.): This method is the most often used Multi-Task Learning approach, which is a weighting strategy that consists in analysing the uncertainty of each task. In this method, each of the task's weights is adjusted by deriving a multi-task loss function when maximising the Gaussian likelihood (Ruder, 2017).

4.3 Hybrid Task Weighting

Among the existing dynamic MTL methods, Uncertainty Weighting (Kendall et al.), and Loss-Balanced Task Weighting (Liu et al., 2019a) both weight all tasks without prioritising on the main task, such that resources are unnecessarily allocated to other tasks, thereby leading to a possible underfitting on the main task (Guo et al.). For this reason, we propose a Hybrid Task Weighting approach, which applies an Abridged Linear schedule for weighting the main task and LBTW (Liu et al., 2019a) for weighting the auxiliary tasks. In particular, for the Abridged Linear schedule, we take a step threshold $t_\tau = T/10$, i.e. 10% of all steps, which is the same as the warm-up ratio we use (see Section 6.4 for further details). To apply LBTW for the auxiliary tasks, a hyperparameter α is used to balance the influence of the task-specific weights, i.e. α=0.5 (Liu et al., 2019a). For each batch, the weight of each task is calculated by using the loss ratio between the loss at step t and the loss at t=0, thereby balancing the loss rates of the auxiliary tasks. Algorithm 1 provides further details about the implementation of our hybrid approach.

5 Research Questions

In this paper, we address two key research questions. Firstly, one of our central contributions is the comparison of existing Multi-Task Learning (MTL) strategies, when used in the same Conversational Question Answering (ConvQA) model both in terms of effectiveness and efficiency. By doing this, we investigate whether there is an actual difference between the static and dynamic loss weighting methods, in guiding the learning process. Moreover, to the best of our knowledge, there has been no previous study that investigated dynamic loss weighting for the ConvQA task on the QuAC dataset. Hence, our first research question is:

RQ1: What is the most effective and efficient Multi-Task Learning method for ConvQA?

Secondly, we investigate the effectiveness of the combination of the auxiliary tasks to improve the performance of the main QuAC task, namely we posit the following research question:

RQ2: Does applying the proposed MTL ConvQA model using each of the auxiliary tasks result in effectiveness improvements over learning using only the main task?

6 Experimental Setup

In this section, we describe the used dataset, QuAC, and its auxiliary tasks in Section 6.1. We present the list of our baselines in Section 6.2. We discuss the used evaluation metrics in Section 6.3, and the applied hyper-parameter settings in Section 6.4.

6.1 Dataset

To conduct our evaluation of the MLT methods when integrated into the BERT ConvQA model, we choose QuAC (Choi et al., 2018), a large-scale dataset for ConvQA over passages extracted from Wikipedia articles. Unlike other Machine Reading datasets such as SQuAD (Rajpurkar et al., 2016, 2018), this dataset is considered to be a multi-turn dataset where the questions and answers simulate conversations. The main reason for choosing this dataset for our experiments is that it provides not only an Answer span prediction as the main task but it also provides other auxiliary tasks namely, the affirmation (Yes/No prediction) and continuation (Follow up prediction) classification tasks. Moreover, we also observe that if an answer in QuAC is tagged as CANNOTANSWER, then this means that the corresponding question cannot be answered. Hence, from these kind of answers, we define another Unanswerable prediction task as an additional auxiliary task to use in our MTL method. We describe below each of the used auxiliary tasks:

Yes/No prediction: This task consists of three possible labels: yes, no, neither where yes or no are represented as the sought answer to this question type; otherwise it will be 'neither'. Choi et al. (2018) observed that there were 25.8% of yes/no questions in the QuAC dataset.

Follow up prediction: This classification task consists in predicting the continuation of a given question, and has three possible labels: follow up, maybe follow up, don't follow up.

Unanswerable prediction: This task has two possible labels: yes/no allocated by inspecting the answer text associated to each question in the dataset. If the answer text is CANNOTANSWER, the label is yes otherwise it is no. 20.2% of all questions in the QuAC dataset are unanswerable.

6.2 Baselines

We use as baselines all methods described in Section 4. Hence, our baselines consist of the Static MTL methods from Section 4.1, namely *sum to 1* and *equal to 1*, and the dynamic MTL methods from Section 4.2, namely Evolving Weighting (Stair, Linear, Abridged Linear, and Exponential), Loss-Balanced Task Weighting, and Uncertainty Weighting as baselines. In addition, we also include Single-Task Learning as a baseline to illustrate the effectiveness of Multi-Task Learning as well as our proposed Hybrid Task Weighting method.

6.3 Evaluation Metrics.

Since we are using the QuAC dataset, we naturally adopt the two evaluation metrics in the corresponding challenge, which consist of the word-level F1, and the human equivalence score (HEQ). The word-level F1, commonly used in Machine Comprehension and in the ConvQA tasks (Rajpurkar et al., 2016, 2018; Choi et al., 2018), evaluates the overlap between the system's prediction and the ground truth answer span. Meanwhile, the HEQ metric is used to evaluate the percentage of examples for which the deployed model's F1 is equivalent to or higher than the human F1. This metric is composed of HEQ-Q, computed on the question level, and HEQ-D, computed at the dialogue level. The QuAC challenge defines the human performance to have an HEQ-Q and HEQ-D of 100%. Finally, we use the McNemar's test to measure statistical significance between the prediction performances.

6.4 Hyper-parameter Settings.

We implement all models using the Pytorch version of BERT from HuggingFace (Wolf et al., 2019), namely using the `bert-base-uncased`[2] model as our encoder. Following Qu et al. (2019b), the model configuration is as follows: the max sequence length is set to 12, the stride in the sliding window is set to 128, the max question length is set to 64, the max answer length set to 35, the number of training epochs is set to 5 and the batch size is set to 12. To train our BERT ConvQA model, we use the BertAdam weight decay optimiser, with an initial learning rate of 5e-5 while the learning rate warming up portion is 10%. For all our experiments, we use a single Nvidia TITAN RTX GPU.

7 Experimental Results

We first report our evaluation results for various MTL methods using our ConvQA model in Section 7.1. Our findings for the usefulness of the auxiliary tasks in MTL are detailed in Section 7.2.

7.1 RQ1: Effectiveness and Efficiency of the MTL Methods

We investigate the performance of the baselines in comparison to our proposed hybrid method for Multi-Task Learning on the validation set[3] of the QuAC dataset. All MTL methods are trained on the provided QuAC training set by using all the auxiliary tasks, namely the Yes/No prediction, the Follow up prediction and the Unanswerable prediction classification tasks. In this section, we focus on the performance of the system on the main task (i.e. the Answer Span prediction task).

First, we examine the effectiveness of the MTL methods, including our proposed methods and those baselines listed in Section 4. Table 2 illustrates the single-task learning baseline (denoted STL) in the first column and the MTL methods in the following columns. Within Table 2, the best result in each row is highlighted in bold. From this table, we observe that the F1 performance of all the MTL methods is better than the STL baseline. Indeed, our proposed method, Hybrid Task Weighting, achieves the best F1 and HEQ-Q performances, at 72.28 and 68.71, respectively. The best reported HEQ-D score is achieved by the Exponential Evolving Weighting method at 13.1 followed by our Hybrid Task Weighting method at 13.0. Indeed, our proposed method is more effective than the Abridged Linear and the Loss-Balanced Task Weighting dynamic methods, showing that while it emphasises the main tasks (c.f. Abridged Linear), it also balances the auxiliary tasks through use of the LBTW method. Moreover, all of the dynamic task weighting methods significantly outperform the STL model, except for the Stair and Uncertainty Weighting methods (McNemar's test, $p < 0.05$).

Next, we investigate the efficiency of the tested MTL methods by comparing the average number of iterations per second needed during training and evaluation. Table 3 depicts the efficiency of the MTL methods for the BERT ConvQA model. In this table, the higher the number, the higher the efficiency, while the best result is highlighted in bold. We observe that the Linear Evolving Weighting yields the best efficiency in comparison to all other methods – at 2.31 iterations per second during learning – while the static task weighting method (equal to 1) exhibits the best evaluation efficiency

Overall the efficiency of most models during

[2] https://huggingface.co/transformers/pretrained_models.html

[3] QuAC's test set is only accessible by submitting to their leaderboard. Hence, we provide results using the provided validation set.

Table 2: Effectiveness of various task-weighting methods for Conversational Question Answering. † denotes a result statistically different from that of our proposed Hybrid Task Weighting model (McNemar's test, $p < 0.05$); ‡ denotes a significant improvement over the STL baseline. The highest value for each measure is highlighted.

	Single-task learning	Static task weighting		Evolving Weighting				Loss-Balanced Task Weighting	Uncertainty Weighting	Hybrid Task Weighting
		Sum to 1	Eq.1	Linear	Exponential	Abridged Linear	Stair			
F1	69.08 †	69.56 †	69.40 †	70.97 †‡	71.16 †‡	71.37 †‡	69.73 †	69.41 †‡	69.20 †	**72.28** ‡
HEQ-Q	65.51	66.06	65.65	67.49	67.88	67.78	66.24	65.71	65.43	**68.71**
HEQ-D	11.6	11.10	10.7	12.8	**13.1**	12.10	11.80	11.6	11.3	13.00

Table 3: Efficiency of different MTL methods. The highest value for each phase is highlighted.

Model		#iters/sec Training	#iters/sec Evaluating
Single-task learning		2.23	3.95
Static task weigthing	Sum to 1.	2.13	4.05
	All eq. 1	2.25	**4.12**
Evolving Weighting	Linear	**2.31**	3.99
	Exponential	2.26	3.90
	Abridged Linear	2.20	3.84
	Stair	2.15	4.07
Loss-Balanced Task Weighting		2.05	3.91
Uncertainty Weighting		1.5	3.94
Hybrid Task Weighting		2.04	4.04

Table 4: Comparison of different combinations of auxiliary tasks. † denotes a statistically significant improvement over STL with $p < 0.05$ using the McNemar's test. The highest value for each measure is highlighted.

	F1	HEQ-Q	HEQ-D
STL	69.08	65.51	11.6
Yes/No	68.60	64.98	11.6
Follow up	69.76 †	66.74	12.0
Unanswerable	72.27 †	68.87	13.5
Yes/No + Follow up	**72.66** †	68.87	11.7
Yes/No + Unanswerable	72.48 †	**69.02**	13.2
Follow up + Unanswerable	71.91 †	68.52	**14.2**
All	72.28 †	68.71	13.0

evaluation is fairly similar, at around 3.8 to 4.1 iterations per second. We argue that this is because during the evaluation phase, all models have the same structure, and only differ in terms of weights. On the other hand, during learning, the Evolving Weighting method is slightly faster than the other baseline methods including our own proposed method due to the simple manner in which it calculates the task weight. Moreover, training the ConvQA model using the Uncertainty Weighting method exhibits more training time than other methods. Indeed, this approach has the most complex implementation.

In response to RQ1, we find that our BERT ConvQA model learned through Multi-Task Learning by using a hybrid approach has the best effectiveness, yielding statistically significant improvements over the baselines. Moreover, we observe that there is little difference between the efficiency of our proposed method, and that of the static task weighting methods, or the single-task learning in both the training and evaluation phases even though our approach has a more complex implementation.

7.2 RQ2: Combination of Auxiliary Tasks vs. Single-Task Learning

Next, we conduct experiments to determine the best combination of auxiliary tasks, which helps to improve the performance of the main task. In these experiments, all models are learned by using our proposed method as the Multi-Task Learning strategy for the BERT ConvQA model. We vary the choice of auxiliary tasks from those detailed in Section 6.1, namely Yes/No prediction, Follow up prediction and Unanswerable prediction. Single-task learning acts as a baseline for these experiments.

Table 4 presents the effectiveness of the different combinations of auxiliary tasks (each row is a different combination). We observe that the highest scores for the F1, HEQ-Q and HEQ-D measures are not obtained from the same combination. In particular, applying Multi-Task Learning using the Yes/No and Follow up tasks achieves the best F1 performance compared to the other combinations. However, when using the HEQ-Q metric, it is apparent that the combination of the Yes/No prediction and Unanswerable prediction is the best. Furthermore, the combination of the Follow up prediction and Unanswerable prediction yields the best model in terms of the HEQ-D metric. From these results, we further analyse why the models that include Unanswerable prediction as one of the auxiliary tasks, have higher HEQ scores in comparison to models that use either the Yes/No prediction or the Follow up prediction as the auxiliary tasks. We found that a key issue is the number of correct predictions for the unanswerable questions. The more correct answers achieved on this type of questions, the more likely the performance will be higher in terms of HEQ. From the table, we also observe that the model that fused all the auxiliary tasks is not the best choice for MTL, and its performance on all metrics is similar to the model that used only the Unanswerable prediction auxiliary task.

In answer to RQ2, we conclude that most of the combination models are better than just learning the main task, except the model that solely used the Yes/No prediction as an auxiliary task. This raises the question as to why the model that combines all the auxiliary tasks does not outperform the models that includes Unanswerable as an auxiliary task. We conjecture that negative transfer (see Section 4.2) might be a possible reason explaining the drop in the performance of MTL. We leave the investigation of this issue to future work.

8 Conclusions

We have proposed a method for Conversational Question Answering, which learns to predict the correct answer span, by applying Multi-Task Learning (MTL). Our proposed hybrid MTL method makes use of Evolving Weighting by Abridged Linear for learning the main task, while the auxiliary tasks are addressed using Loss-Balanced Task Weighting. Our experiments on the QuAC dataset demonstrated that our ConvQA model learned through Multi-Task Learning by using a hybrid approach has the best effectiveness, yielding statistically significant improvements over the baselines. Furthermore, we showed that the use of a combination of the auxiliary tasks resulted in an enhancement to the main task performance compared to single-task learning. For future work, we plan to consider the integration of a question re-writer as well as the use of an attention mechanism for capturing the dialog context.

References

Soufiane Belharbi, Romain Hérault, Clément Chatelain, and Sébastien Adam. 2016. Deep multi-task learning with evolving weights. In *Proc. ESANN*.

Zhao Chen, Vijay Badrinarayanan, Chen-Yu Lee, and Andrew Rabinovich. 2018. GradNorm: Gradient normalization for adaptive loss balancing in deep multitask networks. In *Proc. ICML*, pages 794–803.

Eunsol Choi, He He, Mohit Iyyer, Mark Yatskar, Wentau Yih, Yejin Choi, Percy Liang, and Luke Zettlemoyer. 2018. QuAC: Question answering in context. In *Proc. EMNLP.*, page 2174–2184.

Jacob Devlin, Ming-Wei Chang, Kenton Lee, and Kristina Toutanova. 2019. BERT: Pre-training of deep bidirectional transformers for language understanding. *Proc. NAACL*, pages 4171–4186.

Michelle Guo, Albert Haque, De-An Huang, Serena Yeung, and Li Fei-Fei. Dynamic task prioritization for multitask learning. In *Proc. ECCV*, pages 270–287.

Qiong Hu, Zhizheng Wu, Korin Richmond, Junichi Yamagishi, Yannis Stylianou, and Ranniery Maia. 2015. Fusion of multiple parameterisations for DNN-based sinusoidal speech synthesis with multitask learning. In *Proc. Interspeech*, pages 854–858.

Alex Kendall, Yarin Gal, and Roberto Cipolla. Multitask learning using uncertainty to weigh losses for scene geometry and semantics. In *Proc. CVPR*, pages 7482–7491.

Isabelle Leang, Ganesh Sistu, Fabian Burger, Andrei Bursuc, and Senthil Yogamani. 2020. Dynamic task weighting methods for multi-task networks in autonomous driving systems. *arXiv preprint arXiv:2001.02223*.

Shengchao Liu, Yingyu Liang, and Anthony Gitter. 2019a. Loss-balanced task weighting to reduce negative transfer in multi-task learning. In *Proc. AAAI*, volume 33, pages 9977–9978.

Xiaodong Liu, Jianfeng Gao, Xiaodong He, Li Deng, Kevin Duh, and Ye-yi Wang. 2015. Representation learning using multi-task deep neural networks for semantic classification and information retrieval. In *Proc. NAACL*, pages 912–921.

Xiaodong Liu, Pengcheng He, Weizhu Chen, and Jianfeng Gao. 2019b. Multi-task deep neural networks for natural language understanding. In *Proc. ACL*, pages 4487–4496.

Zuheng Ming, Junshi Xia, Muhammad Muzzamil Luqman, Jean-Christophe Burie, and Kaixing Zhao. 2019. Dynamic Multi-Task Learning for Face Recognition with Facial Expression. In *Proc. ICCV*.

Chen Qu, Liu Yang, Minghui Qiu, W. Bruce Croft, Yongfeng Zhang, and Mohit Iyyer. 2019a. Bert with history answer embedding for conversational question answering. In *Proc. SIGIR*, pages 1133–1136.

Chen Qu, Liu Yang, Minghui Qiu, Yongfeng Zhang, Cen Chen, W. Bruce Croft, and Mohit Iyyer. 2019b. Attentive history selection for conversational question answering. In *Proc. CIKM*, pages 1391–1400.

Pranav Rajpurkar, Robin Jia, and Percy Liang. 2018. Know what you don't know: Unanswerable questions for SQuAD. In *Proc. ACL*, pages 784–789.

Pranav Rajpurkar, Jian Zhang, Konstantin Lopyrev, and Percy Liang. 2016. Squad: 100,000+ questions for machine comprehension of text. In *Proc.EMNLP*, page 2383–2392.

Siva Reddy, Danqi Chen, and Christopher D Manning. 2019. CoQA: A conversational question answering challenge. *Transactions of the Association for Computational Linguistics*, pages 249–266.

Sebastian Ruder. 2017. An overview of multi-task learning in deep neural networks. *arXiv preprint arXiv:1706.05098*.

Thomas Wolf, Lysandre Debut, Victor Sanh, Julien Chaumond, Clement Delangue, Anthony Moi, Pierric Cistac, Tim Rault, Rémi Louf, Morgan Funtowicz, et al. 2019. Huggingface's transformers: State-of-the-art natural language processing. *arXiv preprint arXiv:1910.03771*.

Zhizheng Wu, Cassia Valentini-Botinhao, Oliver Watts, and Simon King. 2015. Deep neural networks employing multi-task learning and stacked bottleneck features for speech synthesis. In *Proc. ICASSP*, pages 4460–4464.

Yichong Xu, Xiaodong Liu, Yelong Shen, Jingjing Liu, and Jianfeng Gao. 2019. Multi-task learning with sample re-weighting for machine reading comprehension. In *Proc. NAACL*, pages 2644–2655.

Yi-Ting Yeh and Yun-Nung Chen. 2019. FlowDelta: Modeling flow information gain in reasoning for conversational machine comprehension. In *Proc. MRQA*, pages 86–90.

Yu Zhang and Qiang Yang. 2017. A survey on multi-task learning. *arXiv preprint arXiv:1707.08114*.

Chenguang Zhu, Michael Zeng, and Xuedong Huang. 2018. SDNet: Contextualized attention-based deep network for conversational question answering. *arXiv preprint arXiv:1812.03593*.

Association for Computational Linguistics
209 N. Eighth Street
Stroudsburg, Pennsylvania 18360

ISBN 978-1-7138-2002-4

CURRAN ASSOCIATES INC.
proceedings.com